Charmaine DellaBella

Teach Yourself
FOUNDATION
PIECING

by Linda Causce

Created for Leisure Arts by The Creative Partners™

Carol Wilson Mansfield, Photo Stylist

Wayne Norton, Photography

Ann Harnden, Copy Editor

Graphic Solutions inc-chgo, Book Design

Produced by The Creative Partners™

Thank you to the talented pattern testers who pieced the projects: Kathryn Causee, Ann Harnden, April McArthur, Kerry Smith, John Schiller, Glenda Tucker and especially, Faith Horsky for her fine machine quilting.

Special thanks to FreeSpirit® for providing fabric and Fairfield Processing Corp. for supplying Cotton Classic® batting for the projects.

CONTENTS

Introduction

If you haven't enjoyed quiltmaking because you find it tedious to use templates, to measure and cut multitudes of squares and triangles, and then hopefully sew everything together accurately, this is the book for you!

Welcome to the world of foundation piecing; no templates here, and even the smallest pieces can be accurately sewn, and every piece meets every other piece precisely and quickly.

In foundation piecing, patchwork is sewn onto a foundation (either paper or fabric) following a numerical sequence. As much as I'd like to say that I invented this technique, the process of using a base for piecing a quilt block is not new. For generations, quilters have used newspaper bases to make string quilts, and the method we call "English Piecing" consists of sewing fabric around a paper base. Crazy quilt foundations were almost always sewn onto muslin or paper. A friend once confirmed the date of a quilt by carefully pulling away the backing to reveal the paper foundation that had been made from a local newspaper that displayed the date the paper had been published.

Now with this book, you can teach yourself to make quilts quickly and exactly. It's fun! Before beginning, read the general directions which start on page five. Then decide which quilt you are going to make. The quilts in this collection are arranged according to difficulty, starting with the easy ones and progressing to the more difficult. As much as you may desire to plow right in and make the most difficult quilt first, it might be a good idea to start with a simple one.

If you are not too sure of your hand piecing ability, or you are not too friendly with your sewing machine, why not try making just one of the blocks. "Garden Stars" on page 19 and "Sunny Whirligigs" on page 23 are good beginning projects because the blocks do not contain many pieces. Once you have become more familiar with the foundation-piecing technique, there will be no holding you back.

HOW TO MAKE A FOUNDATION-PIECED QUILT

In Foundation Piecing, the stitching lines are placed onto the foundation. The fabric pieces are placed onto the unmarked side of the foundation and then sewn on the marked side. The technique can be done either by machine or by hand.

WHAT DO I USE FOR A FOUNDATION?

Paper

The first step in foundation piecing is to decide what you are going to use for the foundation on which to piece your quilt. The most popular option is paper: copy paper, newsprint, tracing paper or computer paper. Everyone has paper, and it is readily available. If you are planning to trace your blocks, you will want to use a paper that is thin enough to see through.

Fabric

Another choice is fabric, usually muslin. Use a fabric that is light-colored and lightweight enough to allow you to trace the pattern. The advantage to a fabric base is that it will give your blocks extra stability. Because the fabric is not removed after the block has been pieced, the extra thickness of the fabric can make hand quilting more difficult. If you plan to use muslin, make certain that you use a good quality 100% cotton muslin. If you are unable to find the right kind of muslin, use a white or cream 100% cotton fabric.

Freezer Paper

Freezer paper is a wax-coated paper that was originally found only in the grocery store. Over the past few years as more and more quilters have discovered the advantages of freezer paper, it is now often available at quilt shops. Freezer paper is especially useful for large pieces of fabric that may shift. The foundation is drawn on the uncoated side of the freezer paper. The fabric is placed on the coated side. After the pieces are sewn and flipped over, press with a warm iron and fabric will adhere to freezer paper. You will eliminate the need for pinning or gluing fabric pieces in place. Be sure that you do not touch the iron to any part of the coated side that is not covered with fabric.

Other Methods

Tear Away® or Fun-dation™ are other foundation options. These are translucent non-woven materials that combine the advantages of both paper and fabric. Like fabric they are easy to see through for tracing but like paper they can easily be removed.

A new kind of foundation material has recently arrived on the market. It is called WashAway™ and is produced by W.H. Collins. After sewing the block, place it in water, and the foundation will disappear in about ten seconds.

Advantages and Disadvantages

Each of the foundation choices has its advantages and disadvantages. Experiment with the choices and decide which one works best for you. Fabric will remain a permanent part of your quilt, while paper and TearAway® will have to be removed, a sometimes very tedious process.

If you use a fabric base, it will remain a part of your quilt, and will add another layer to quilt. The advantage to fabric is that it can be sewn either by hand or machine. If you want to use non-traditional fabrics, such as satins or rayons, the fabric will add stability to the quilt block.

Paper can only be used if you are planning to machine piece your quilt. It is, however, relatively inexpensive and makes hand quilting easier since the foundation has to be removed.

HOW DO I MAKE THE FOUNDATION?

Tracing

Using a ruler and a fine-point marker or a fine mechanical pencil, carefully trace the block patterns from this book on to your foundation material. (Short dashed lines or even dotted lines are easier to make than perfect straight lines. Just be sure they are straight and accurate.) Repeat the process for the required number of blocks for your quilt. If you find it difficult to see the block through your foundation material, try tracing the block initially onto tracing paper.

Transfer Pens

Several companies currently market transfer pens and pencils. Be sure to experiment until you find one that works for you. Using tracing paper, transfer the design with the transfer pen. Then following the manufacturer's instructions, use a hot iron to transfer the block onto your foundation paper or fabric. Repeat the process for the required number of blocks. Transfer pens can be used for several blocks. Note that your finished block will be a mirror image of the finished blocks shown in our quilts. To avoid this, you will need to trace the block first onto tracing paper with a permanent pen, then flop the traced block and retrace using the transfer pen.

Copiers

If you have access to a copy machine, you can copy the block from the book directly onto paper that can be used for your foundation. Just remember to copy each block from the original pattern rather than from another copied block. The copy machine could alter the measurements of the block slightly. This won't matter so long as each block is the same.

Scanners and Printers

If you have a printer and a scanner, you can scan the block, and then print out the number of blocks that are required. It is even possible to print on muslin if it is first ironed onto freezer paper.

No matter which method you use, be sure to copy the numbers as well as the letters for the blocks that require multiple sections. Make certain that the block pattern is accurate and that the ink on the foundation is permanent and will not rub off onto your fabric if using a paper foundation or wash into your fabric if using a muslin foundation.

WHAT SHOULD I KNOW ABOUT THE FABRIC FOR MY QUILT?

For several hundred years, quilts were made with 100% cotton fabric, and this remains the fabric of choice for most quilters today.

There are many properties in cotton that make it especially well suited for foundation piecing. There is less distortion in cotton fabric, thereby affording the foundation piecer greater security in making certain that the smallest pieces will not slip as easily and will respond better to finger pressing. The sewing machine needle can move through cotton with a great deal of ease as compared to synthetic fabrics. While you may find that some foundation piecers today use other kinds of fabric, 100% cotton is strongly recommended, especially for beginners.

For years, quilters were advised to prewash all of their fabric to test for colorfastness and shrinkage. Now most quilters don't bother to prewash all of their fabric, but they do pre-test. If you are using scraps of fabric from other projects, it is assumed that those fabrics have been tested and found workable so testing at this time will not be required.

To test, cut a strip about 2" wide from each piece of fabric that you will use. Measure both the length and the width of the strip, and then immerse the strip in a bowl of very hot water. Use a separate bowl for each piece of fabric.

Be especially concerned about reds and dark blues because they have a tendency to bleed if the initial dyeing was not done correctly. If one of your favorite fabrics bleeds, you might be able to salvage the fabric. Try washing the fabric in very hot water until you've washed out all of the excess dye. Unfortunately, fabrics that continue to bleed after they have been washed repeatedly will bleed forever. So, eliminate them immediately

To test for shrinkage, take each one of the strips used in the color test and iron them dry using a hot iron. Be especially careful not to stretch the strip. When the strips are completely dry, measure them to your original strip. If all of your fabric is shrinking the same amount, you don't have to worry about uneven shrinkage in your quilt. When you wash the final quilt, the puckering that may result will give you the look of an antique quilt. If you don't want this look, you will have to wash and dry all of your fabric before starting to cut. If some of the fabric shrinks more than others, you may have to prewash or discard the errant fabric.

If you are never planning to wash your quilt because the quilt is intended to be a wall hanging, you could eliminate the pre-testing process. You may run the risk, however, of some future relative to whom you have willed your quilt collection deciding that the wall hanging needs freshening by washing.

When preparing fabric for traditional quilting, it is important to make certain that the fabric is absolutely square. Otherwise it is difficult to cut perfectly square pieces. In foundation piecing, making certain that the fabric is square is not as important because the foundation itself provides a certain amount of stability to the blocks. It doesn't hurt, however, to try to get the fabric square, especially for cutting borders. Fabric is woven with crosswise and lengthwise threads. Lengthwise threads should be parallel to the selvage (that's the finished edge along the sides; sometimes the fabric company prints its name along the selvage), and crosswise threads should be perpendicular to the selvage. If the fabric is off-grain, you can usually straighten it by pulling gently on the true bias in the opposite direction to the off-grain. Continue doing this until the crosswise threads are at a right angle to the lengthwise threads. The lengthwise grain has the least stretch; it is therefore helpful to have this lengthwise grainline at the outside edge of the block. If you have sufficient yardage, it's a good idea to cut your borders along the lengthwise grainline.

Cutting the Fabric

The greatest advantage of foundation piecing is that you do not have to cut perfectly exact pieces. You can use squares, strips, rectangles or odd pieces for piecing. You will enjoy this advantage when you work with blocks that have many small pieces. It's much easier to handle even small pieces of fabric than it is to perfectly piece tiny triangles that must meet.

The one thing to remember about cutting the fabric is that all pieces must be at least ¼" larger on all sides than the space they are going to cover. It's very easy to figure strips and squares. Just measure the width and length of the space, add ½" and cut your strip to that measurement. For your convenience, the widths of the strips are given in the Cutting Instructions with each project. Cut fabrics into strips as needed. Triangles are a bit trickier. Measure the widest point of the triangle, and cut your fabric about ½" to 1" wider. In the beginning, you may be safer if you cut generous pieces of fabric. **(Diagram 1)**

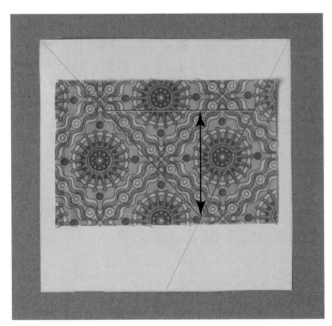

Diagram 1

WHAT OTHER SUPPLIES DO I NEED?

For Foundation Piecing by hand: You will only need a needle, thread, some pins, a glue stick, a pair of fabric scissors, muslin or fabric for foundation bases and some fabric. For sewing the blocks, any reasonably thin needle such as a Sharp, size 10 will do. Any good-quality thread will work, but a size 50 cotton is probably best. (The higher the number on the spool of thread or the needles, the thinner or finer the thread and the smaller the needle.) A neutral color thread, such as a medium-gray or a beige, works for most projects. If you are working with a block that uses a one-color family, then naturally you will want to piece with a medium-color thread of that family.

For Foundation Piecing by machine: You will need a sewing machine that is in good running order. Make sure that the machine has been recently cleaned and oiled. If the needle has not been changed in a while, now would be the time to change it. Many quilters use a new needle with every quilt. Wind a few bobbins with the thread you are planning to use (a good-quality thread is the best). Put a lighter thread in the bobbin and a darker thread in the top,

You will also need a glue stick, some pins, a pair of paper scissors (if you are piecing on paper) and a pair of sharp scissors for cutting fabric plus your choice of foundation material.

If you use paper as your foundation, a good idea would be to determine your stitch length before you begin sewing the actual block. Take a piece of the paper you are planning to use for your foundation and draw a straight line on it. Then set your machine so that it is sewing with a short stitch—about 20 stitches per inch—and sew along the line. If you are able to tear the paper apart easily—provided it doesn't simply fall apart by itself—you will be sewing with the correct length. Sewing with the small stitch will make it easier to remove the paper, but if the stitch is too small, the paper will fall apart after stitching. It is important to adjust your stitch length before you start.

If you are planning to use a fabric foundation, use the stitch length that you normally use for sewing on your machine. You may find that a slightly shorter length—about 12 to 14 stitches to the inch—will work better.

WHERE ARE THE PATTERNS FOR THE QUILT BLOCKS?

In this book, you will find patterns for the blocks that make up the quilts. The block patterns range in size from 6" to 10" finished, but the finished blocks can be as large as 20". The numbers on the block patterns show the order in which the pieces are to be placed and sewn on the base. The entire process won't work if you don't follow the numbers.

The easier blocks, which appear first, have only one section. The later quilts have blocks which have more than one section. The sections—indicated by letters—must be individually pieced and then sewn together. A bold line indicates the cutting line for these sections. If you have never made a foundation-pieced quilt, start with the easier blocks.

Because you sew on one side of the foundation and place the fabric on the other side, what you see on the printed side is not what you get on the fabric side. The finished blocks will be mirror images of the original patterns. **(Diagram 2)**

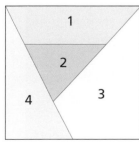 

Block Pattern   Finished Block

Diagram 2

HOW DO I MAKE THE BLOCK?

Prepare your foundation as described on page 6 under How Do I Make the Foundation?.

Blocks that have two or more sections will need to be cut along the bold lines. **(Diagram 3)**

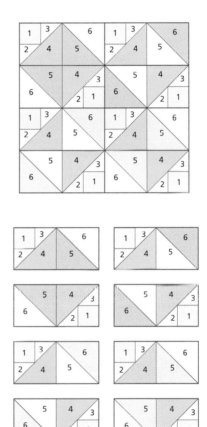

Diagram 3

When making foundation-pieced blocks, the important thing to remember is that the fabric pieces go on the unmarked side of the foundation, and you sew on the printed side.

9

Hold your foundation up to a light source (a window pane works) with the unmarked side facing you. Find Space #1 on the unmarked side and put a tiny bit of glue there. Place Piece #1 with the fabric right side up on the unmarked side on Space #1. Make sure that your fabric overlaps at 1/4" on all sides of Space #1. **(Diagram 4)**

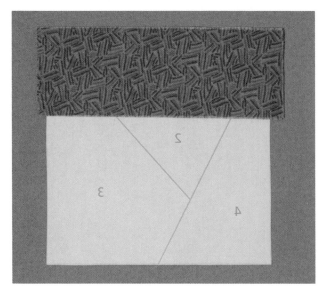

Diagram 4

Now fold the foundation back along the line between Space # 1 and Space #2. Cut the fabric so that it is 1/4" from the fold. **(Diagram 5)**

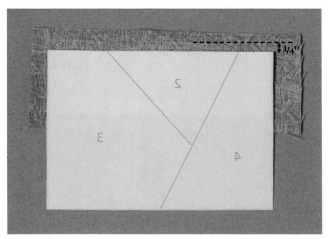

Diagram 5

Take Fabric Piece #2 and place it right sides together with Piece #1. Make sure that the edge of Piece #2 is even with the edge of Piece #1 that has just been trimmed. **(Diagram 6)**

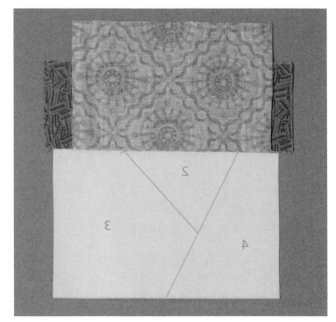

Diagram 6

Check to make sure that Piece #2 will cover Space #2 by folding fabric piece back over along the line between Space #1 and Space #2. **(Diagram 7)**

Diagram 7

10

Making sure that the marked side of the foundation is facing you, place the piece on your sewing machine, (or sew by hand) holding Piece #1 and Piece #2 in place. Sew along the line between Space #1 and Space #2. **(Diagram 8)** **Note:** *Using a very small stitch will make it easier to remove the paper later. Remember that if your paper falls apart as you sew, you will need to lengthen the stitch slightly.* Start your stitching about two or three stitches before the beginning of the line and end two or three stitches beyond the end of the line. This will allow your threads to be anchored by the subsequent stitching. Don't backstitch because this can sometimes lead to stitching that is not exactly on the line and it will add bulk to the seam allowance especially where points meet.

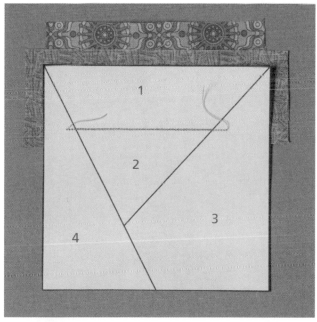

Diagram 8

Turn the work over, and open Piece #2. **(Diagram 9)** Finger press the seam open. If you are concerned that fabric may not stay in place, pin it, or dab it with a bit of glue stick.

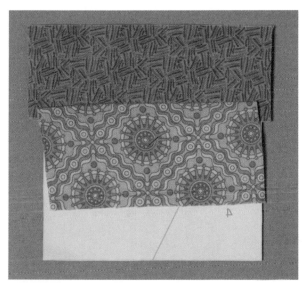

Diagram 9

Now turn the work so that the marked side is facing you, and fold the foundation forward along the line between Space #1/2 and Space #3. Trim about 1/8" to 1/4" from the fold. **(Diagram 10)** If you are using paper for your foundation, it will make it easier to trim if you pull the paper away from the stitching. If you are using fabric, fold the fabric forward as far as it will go before you start to trim.

Diagram 10

Place Fabric #3 right side down and even with the edge that has just been trimmed. **(Diagram 11)**

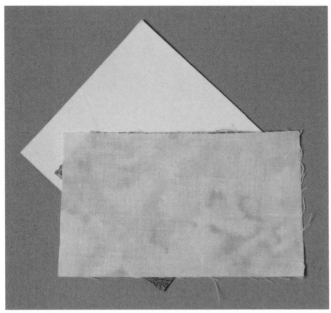

Diagram 11

Turn the work over. Open Piece #3 and finger press the seam. If necessary, glue or pin it in place. **(Diagram 13)**

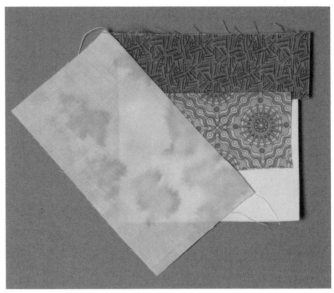

Diagram 13

Turn the work over to the marked side and sew along the line between Space #1/2 and Space #3. **(Diagram 12)**

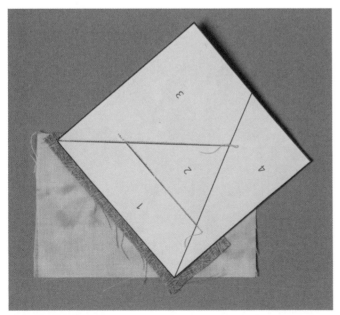

Diagram 12

Add Piece #4 in same manner to complete the block. Trim the fabric ¼" from the edge of the foundation. **(Diagram 14)**

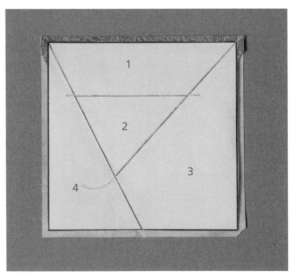

Diagram 14

After you have completed a block, resist the temptation to remove the paper. Since grainline was not considered in cutting the pieces, many of the pieces will be on the bias, and they will have a tendency to stretch. If you keep the paper in place until all of the blocks are sewn together, you will eliminate distortion.

If you are determined to remove the paper, stay stitch along the outer edge of the block. This will help keep the block in shape. **(Diagram 15)**

Diagram 15

A number of the blocks in this collection have two or more sections, which are indicated by dark lines. The sections are made independently, and then must be sewn together. Before you begin to piece the block, cut the foundation piece apart so that each section may be worked on independently.

When each section has been completed, place the sections right sides together. Push a pin from the corner of the top section to the corner of the bottom section. Repeat at the opposite corner to match the seams. **(Diagram 16)**

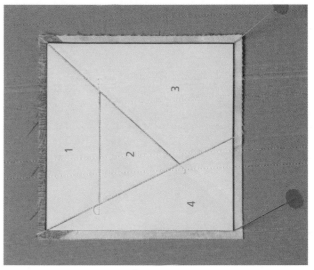

Diagram 16

When you have determined that the pieces are lined up correctly, using the regular stitch length on your machine, sew the two sections together. **(Diagram 17)**

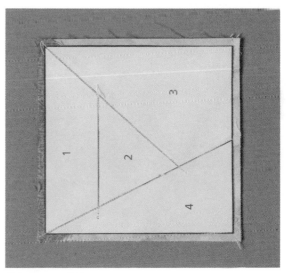

Diagram 17

13

Press sections open and continue sewing sections in pairs. **(Diagram 18)**

Diagram 18

Sew pairs of sections together to complete block. **(Diagram 19)**

Diagram 19

HOW DO I MAKE A COMPLETE QUILT?

Making the Top

Following the instructions given with each quilt, make the number of blocks that are needed for the quilt. Using the layout plan as a guide, lay out the blocks. Sew the blocks together in rows, and press the seams for the rows in alternate directions. Matching the seams, sew the rows together

Most of the quilts in this collection have borders added to the top, sides and bottom of the quilts. To add borders, measure the quilt top lengthwise through the center and cut two border strips to that length by the width measurement given in the instructions. Sew both strips to the sides of the quilt.

Now measure the quilt top crosswise through the center, being sure to include the measurement of the borders you have just added. Cut two border strips, following the width measurement given in the instructions. Add these borders to the top and bottom of the quilt. Repeat this process for any additional borders. Use a ¼" seam allowance at all times and press all of the seams toward the border just added. Press the quilt top carefully,

Sometimes border strips will have to be pieced to achieve the correct length. Sew strips together diagonally to make the seam less noticeable.

Attaching the Batting and Backing

There are a number of different types of batting on the market today, including the new fusible battings that eliminate the need for basting. Your choice of batting will depend upon how you are planning to use your quilt. If your quilt is to serve as a wall hanging, you will probably want to use a thin cotton batting. Batting made with a thin cotton or cotton/polyester blend works best for machine quilting. Very thick polyester batting should be used only for tied quilts.

It is a good idea to remove the batting from its wrapping 24 hours before you plan to use it and open it out to full size. You will find that the batting will now lie flat when you are ready to use it.

The best fabric for quilt backing is 100% cotton fabric. If your quilt is larger than the available fabric you will have to piece your backing fabric. When joining the fabric, try not to have a seam going down the center. Instead cut off the selvages and make a center strip that is about 36" wide and have narrower strips at the sides. Seam the pieces together and carefully iron the seams open. (This is one of the few times in making a quilt that a seam should be pressed open.) Several fabric manufacturers are now selling fabric in 90" or 108"-widths for use as backing fabric.

The batting and the backing should be cut about one to two inches larger on all sides than the quilt top. Place the backing wrong side up on a flat surface. Smooth out the batting on top of this, matching the outer edges. Center the quilt top, right side up, on top of the batting.

WHAT ARE SOME OF THE THINGS I NEED TO REMEMBER ABOUT FOUNDATION PIECING?

- When sewing by hand, take some backstitches to anchor the thread, then start sewing at the beginning of the line and sew to the end with small running stitches. Make a backstitch every four or five stitches, and sew tightly enough so that the thread will not show through when you open the fabric piece. Don't sew so tightly that you gather your fabric foundation. End the stitching with a few backstitches.

- When sewing by machine, start your stitching about two or three stitches before the beginning of the stitching line and end your stitching two or three stitches after the end of the stitching line.

- If you are using paper foundations, use a short stitch (about 20 stitches per inch) in order to make it easier to remove the paper. If the paper rips as you sew, slightly lengthen the stitch.

- As you finish each seam, finger press or press with an iron.

- Never fear if your stitching goes through a whole space into another space. That won't interfere with adding additional fabric pieces.

- Trim all seam allowances at least 1/4".

- If you are sewing points, it is easier to start from the wide end and sew towards the point.

- As a rule, don't use directional prints in foundation piecing unless the print is used only once in the block.

- Don't worry about grainline.

- Always remember that you sew on the marked side, but place the fabric on the unmarked side.

- Always follow the numerical order.

- After you have finished sewing a block, do not remove the paper unless you stay stitch around the outside of a block. Wait until the entire quilt has been completed to remove the papers.

- Make certain that the ink used on your foundation is permanent and will not rub off or wash out into your fabric.

Now the quilt layers must be held together before quilting, and there are several methods for doing this:

Safety-pin Basting: Starting from the center and working toward the edges, pin through all layers at one time with large safety pins. The pins should be placed no more than 4" apart. As you work, think of your quilting plan to make sure that the pins will avoid prospective quilting lines.

Thread Basting: Baste the three layers together with long stitches. Start in the center and sew toward the edges in a number of diagonal lines.

Quilt-gun Basting: This handy trigger tool pushes nylon tags through all layers of the quilt. Start in the center and work toward the outside edges. The tags should be placed about 4" apart. You can sew right over the tags, which can then be easily removed by cutting them off with scissors.

Spray or Heat-Set Basting: Several manufacturers have spray adhesives available especially for quilters. Apply these products by following the manufacturers' directions. You might want to test these products before you use them to make sure that they meet your requirements.

Fusible Iron-on Batting: These battings are a great new way to hold quilt layers together without using the other time-consuming methods of basting. Again, you will want to test these battings to be certain that you are happy with the results. Follow the manufacturers' directions.

Quilting

If you like the process of hand quilting, you can—of course—finish these projects by hand quilting. However, if you want to finish these quilts quickly, use a sewing machine for quilting.

If you have never used a sewing machine for quilting, you may want to find a book and read about the technique. You do not need a special machine for quilting. Just make sure that your machine has been oiled and is in good working condition.

If you are going to do machine quilting, you should invest in an even-feed foot. This foot is designed to feed the top and bottom layers of a quilt evenly through the machine. The foot prevents puckers from forming as you machine quilt. Use a fine transparent nylon thread in the top and regular sewing thread in the bobbin.

Quilting in the Ditch is one of the easiest ways to machine quilt. This is a term used to describe stitching along the seam line between two pieces of fabric. Using your fingers, pull the blocks or pieces apart slightly and machine stitch right between the two pieces. The stitching will look better if you keep the stitching to the side of the seam that does not have the extra bulk of the seam allowance under it. The quilting will be hidden in the seam.

Free-form Machine Quilting can be used to quilt around a design or to quilt a motif. The quilting is done with a darning foot and the feed dogs down on the sewing machine. It takes practice to master free-form quilting because you are controlling the movement of the quilt under the needle rather than the sewing machine moving the quilt. You can quilt in any direction—up and down, side-to-side and even in circles—without pivoting the quilt around the needle. Practice this quilting method before trying it on your quilt.

Attaching the Continuous Machine Binding

Once the quilt has been quilted, the edges must be bound. Start by trimming the backing and batting even with the quilt top. Measure the quilt top and cut enough 2½"-wide strips to go around all four sides of the quilt plus 12". Join the strips end to end with diagonal seams and trim the corners. **(Diagrams 20 & 21)** Press the seams open.

Diagram 20

Diagram 21

Cut one end of the strip at a 45-degree angle and fold under ¼"; press. **(Diagram 22)**

Diagram 22

Press entire strip in half lengthwise, wrong sides together. **(Diagram 23)**

Diagram 23

On the back of the quilt, position the binding in the middle of one side, keeping the raw edges together. Sew the binding to the quilt with the ¼" seam allowance, beginning about three inches below the folded end of the binding. **(Diagram 24)**

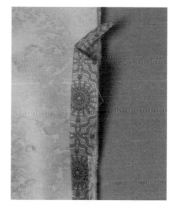

Diagram 24

At the corner, stop ¼" from the edge of the quilt and backstitch. Remove quilt and cut threads.

Fold binding away from quilt so it is at a right angle to the edge just sewn. **(Diagram 25)**

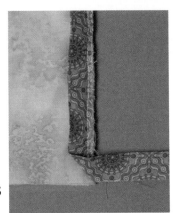

Diagram 25

Fold the binding back on itself so the fold is on the quilt edge and the raw edges are aligned with the adjacent side of the quilt. Begin sewing at the quilt edge. **(Diagram 26)**

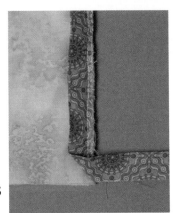

Diagram 26

Continue in the same way around the remaining sides of the quilt. Stop about 2" away from the starting point. Trim any excess binding and tuck

it inside the folded end. Finish the stitching. **(Diagram 27)**

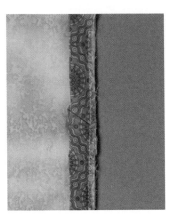

Diagram 27

Fold the binding to the front of the quilt so the seam line is covered; machine-stitch the binding in place on the front of the quilt. Use a straight stitch or tiny zigzag with invisible or matching thread. **(Diagram 28)** If you have a sewing machine that does embroidery stitches, you may want to use your favorite stitch.

Diagram 28

Always sign and date your quilt when finished. You can make a label by cross-stitching or embroidering or even writing on a label or on the back of your quilt with a permanent marking pen. If you are friends with your computer, you can even create an attractive label on the computer.

GARDEN STARS

Because there are only three pieces in each block, this is the perfect quilt to start learning about foundation piecing. Purple and green stars endlessly float across this colorful floral garden. A very simple quilt, Garden Stars can easily be made in a weekend as a special gift for a special person.

Approximate Size: 48½" x 60½"
Block size: 6" finished
Number of Blocks: 63

MATERIALS

2¾ yards floral print
⅜ yard dark green
½ yard light green
½ yard dark purple
⅝ yard light purple
½ yard dark purple (first border)
¾ yard floral print (second border)
½ yard binding fabric
3 yards backing fabric
Batting

CUTTING INSTRUCTIONS

For Foundation piecing, you do not have to cut exact pieces. To make it easier for you, however, I have given you the size to cut squares for each space. This will make piecing easier and may waste less fabric. If you prefer, follow the instructions on page 7 and cut fabric pieces as you sew.

63–6½" squares, floral print
18–4" squares, dark green

28–4" squares, light green
32–4" squares, dark purple
48–4" squares, light purple

Borders, Binding

Six 2½"-wide strips, dark purple (first border)

Seven 3¼"-wide strips, floral print (second border)

Seven 2½"-wide strips, binding fabric

INSTRUCTIONS

Note: Read How Do I Make the Block?, pages 9 to 14, before beginning.

1. Using pattern on page 22, make 63 foundations referring to How Do I Make the Foundation?, page 6.

2. Make 14 blocks with light green corners, 24 with light purple, 16 with dark purple and nine with dark green. **(Diagram 1)**

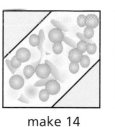
make 14

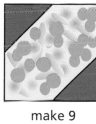
make 9

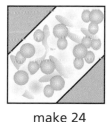
make 24

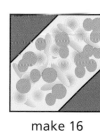
make 16

Diagram 1

3. Place blocks in nine rows of seven blocks referring to Layout.

4. Sew blocks together in rows. Press seams for rows in opposite directions, then sew rows together.

5. Refer to How Do I Make a Complete Quilt?, pages 14 to 18, to add borders and finish your quilt.

Garden Stars Quilt Layout

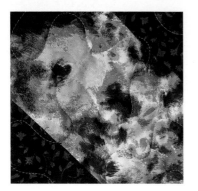

GARDEN STARS
BLOCK PATTERN

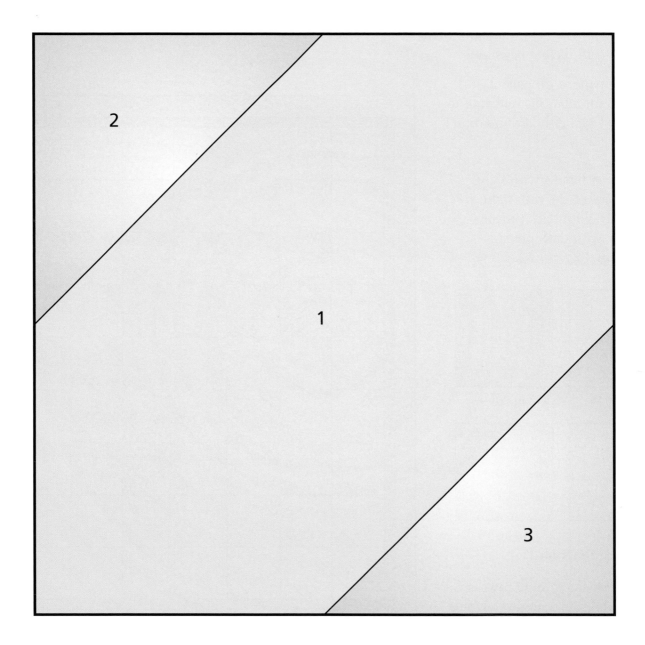

SUNNY WHIRLIGIGS

With only four pieces in each block, this quilt that could be a great beginner's project. When you have put the entire quilt together, bright yellow whirligigs will dance across the quilt, bringing a little sunshine to enhance any room.

Approximate Size: 52" x 66"
Block Size: 14" finished
Number of Blocks: 12

MATERIALS

1 1/2 yards yellow/orange
2 yards yellow/orange/blue
3/4 yard light blue
3/4 yard medium blue
1/2 yard medium blue (first border)
1 yard yellow/orange/blue (second border)
5/8 yard binding fabric
3 yards backing fabric
Batting

CUTTING INSTRUCTIONS

For Foundation piecing, you do not have to cut exact pieces. To make it easier for you, however, I have given you the size to cut strips for each space. This will make piecing easier and may waste less fabric. If you prefer, follow the instructions on page 7 and cut fabric pieces as you sew.

Nine 2 1/2"-wide strips, medium blue (space 1)
Six 3 1/2"-wide strips, light blue (space 2)
Eleven 5 1/4"-wide strips, yellow/orange/blue (space 3)
Eleven 3 3/4"-wide strips, yellow/orange (space 4)

Borders, Binding

Seven 2"-wide strips, medium blue (first border)
Eight 4"-wide strips, yellow/orange/blue (second border)
Eight 2 1/2"-wide strips, binding fabric

INSTRUCTIONS

Note: *Read How Do I Make the Block?, pages 9 to 14, before beginning.*

1. Using pattern on page 27, make 48 foundations referring to How Do I Make the Foundation?, page 6.

2. Make 48 quarter blocks using the Cutting Instructions as a guide. (**Diagram 1**)

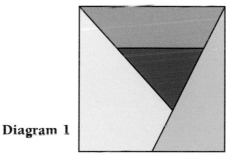

Diagram 1

make 48

23

3. Sew two squares together noting position. (**Diagram 2**)

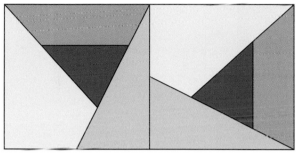

Diagram 2

4. Sew pairs of squares together to complete Whirligig block. (**Diagram 3**) Repeat for 11 more Whirligig blocks.

Diagram 3　　make 12

5. Place blocks in four rows of three blocks referring to Layout on page 26.

6. Sew blocks together in rows. Press seams for rows in opposite directions then sew rows together.

7. Refer to How Do I Make a Complete Quilt?, pages 14 to 18, to add borders and finish your quilt.

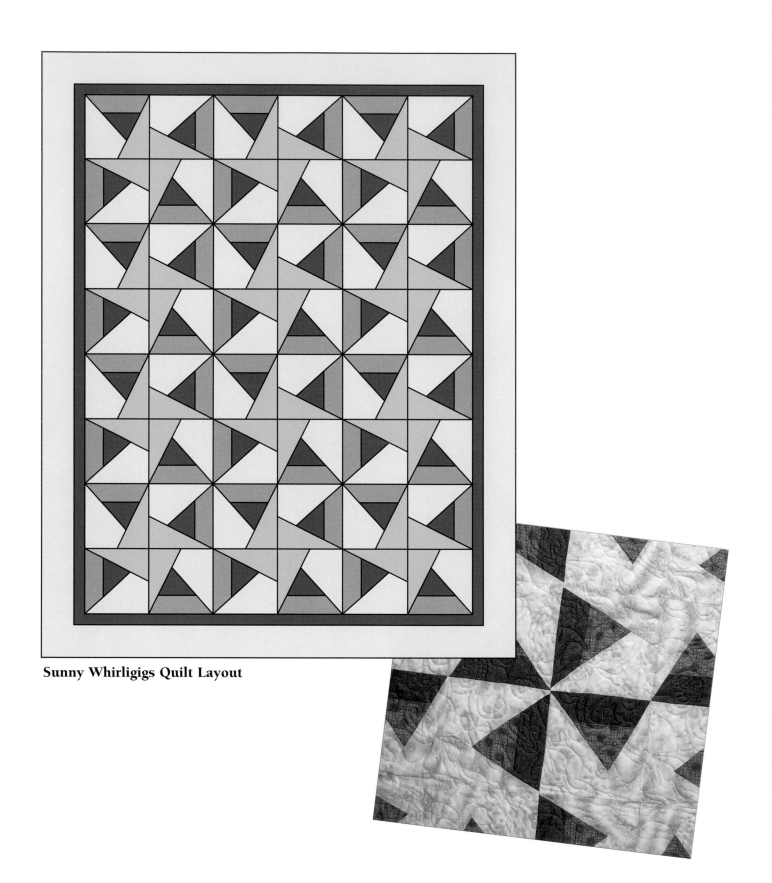

Sunny Whirligigs Quilt Layout

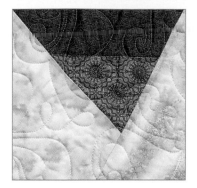

SUNNY WHIRLIGIGS
QUARTER-BLOCK PATTERN

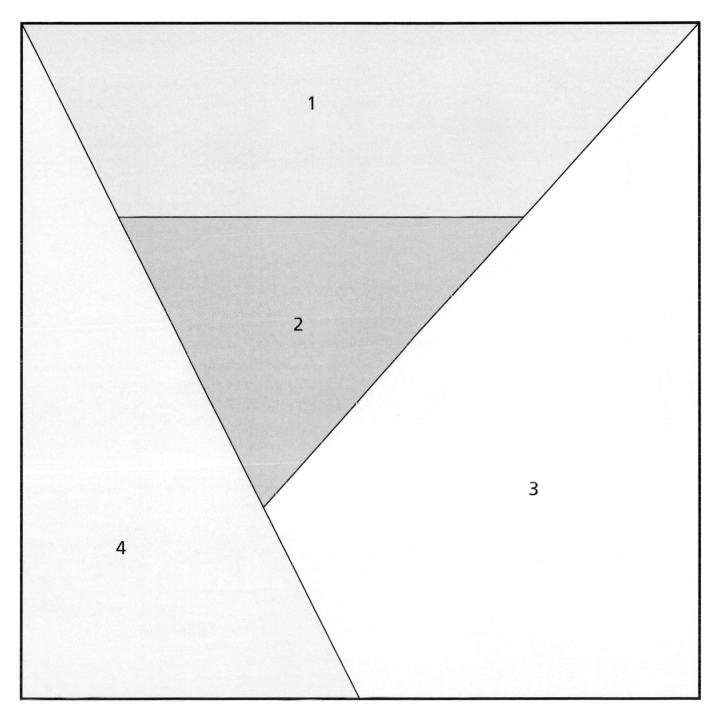

STARRY PINWHEELS

While this quilt may look complicated, it is really quite easy to put together if you follow the plan carefully. Watch the bright cheerful stars appear along small turquoise pinwheels as the blocks go together.

Approximate Size: 48" x 48"
Block Size: 12" finished
Number of Blocks: 9

MATERIALS

1 yard yellow
3/8 yard green
1/4 yard blue
3/8 yard orange
1 yard white
1/4 yard pink
3/8 yard pink (first border)
3/4 yard blue (second border)
1/2 yard binding fabric
2 1/4 yards backing fabric
Batting

CUTTING INSTRUCTIONS

For Foundation piecing, you do not have to cut exact pieces. To make it easier for you, however, I have given you the size to cut strips for each space. This will make piecing easier and may waste less fabric. If you prefer, follow the instructions on page 7 and cut fabric pieces as you sew.

Six 3 7/8"-wide strips, white (spaces 1, 3, 6)
Two 3 7/8"-wide strips, green (space 2)
Two 3 7/8"-wide strips, pink or blue (space 4)

Seven 3 1/2"-wide strips, yellow (space 5)
Two 3 7/8"-wide strips, orange (space 7)

Borders, Binding
Four 2 1/2"-wide strips, pink (first border)
Five 4 1/2"-wide strips, blue (second border)
Six 2 1/2"-wide strips, binding fabric

INSTRUCTIONS

Note: *Read How Do I Make the Block?, pages 9 to 14, before beginning.*

1. Using patterns on page 32 and 33, prepare 36 foundations referring to How Do I Make the Foundation?, page 6.

2. Make 18 Star A blocks with blue in space 4 and 18 Star B with pink in space 4. (**Diagram 1**)

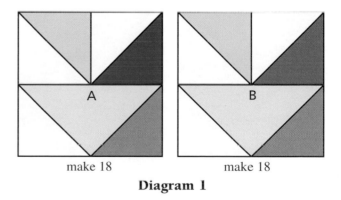

make 18   make 18

Diagram 1

3. Sew Star A to Star B noting position. (**Diagram 2**)

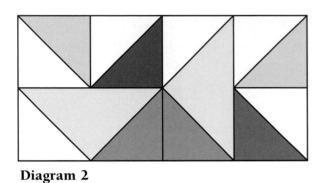

Diagram 2

4. Sew pairs together to complete Star block. (**Diagram 3**)

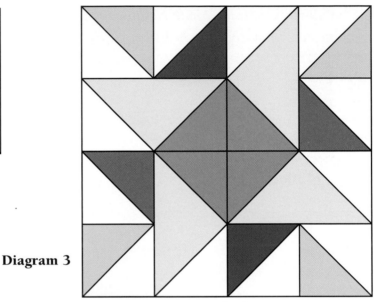

Diagram 3

make 9

5. Repeat steps 3 and 4 for eight more blocks

6. Place blocks in three rows of three blocks each referring to Layout on page 31.

7. Sew blocks together in rows. Press seams for rows in opposite directions then sew rows together.

8. Refer to How Do I Make a Complete Quilt?, pages 14 to 18, to add borders and finish your quilt.

Starry Pinwheels Quilt Layout

STARRY PINWHEELS
BLOCK A PATTERN

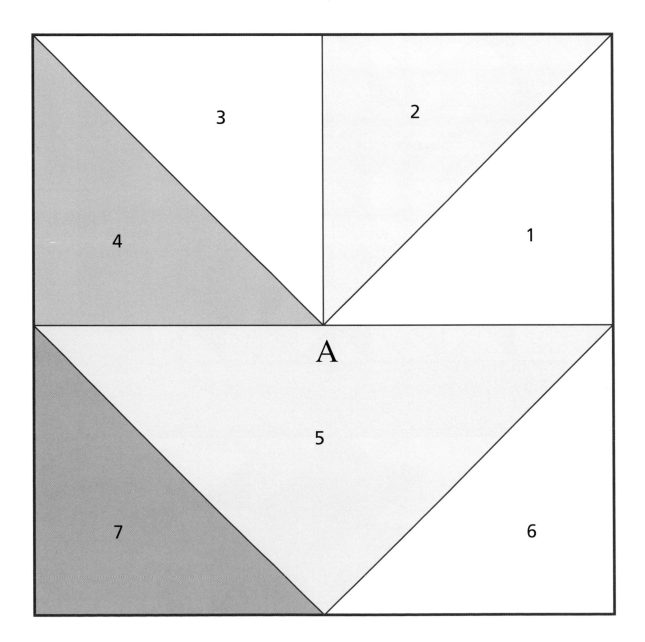

3

2

4

1

A

5

7

6

STARRY PINWHEELS
BLOCK B PATTERN

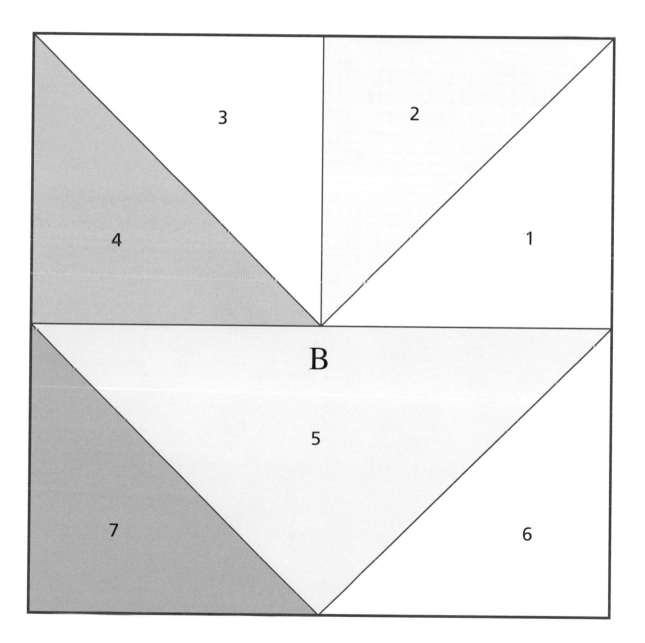

LONDON'S PINWHEELS

A bright colorful kid's print served as the theme fabric in choosing the color scheme for this quilt made for a special little girl named London. Because it is so easy to piece using the foundation method, you might want to make this quilt for all of your favorite little girls.

Approximate Size: 48" x 60"
Block size: 12" finished
Number of Blocks: 12

MATERIALS

1¼ yards yellow
1¼ yards turquoise
⅞ yard orange
⅞ yard purple
⅞ yard white
½ yard purple (first border)
1 yard kid's theme print (second border)
¾ yard binding fabric
3 yards backing fabric
Batting

CUTTING INSTRUCTIONS

For foundation piecing, you do not have to cut exact pieces. To make it easier for you, however, I have given you the size to cut strips for each space. This will make piecing easier and may waste less fabric. If you prefer, follow the instructions on page 7 and cut fabric pieces as you sew.

Block A

Three 4"-wide strips, white (space 1)
Three 4"-wide strips, purple (space 2)
Three 4"-wide strips, orange (space 3)
Three 4"-wide strips, turquoise (space 4)
Five 7"-wide strips, yellow (space 5)

Block B

Three 4"-wide strips, white (space 1)
Three 4"-wide strips, purple (space 2)
Three 4"-wide strips, orange (space 3)
Three 4"-wide strips, yellow (space 4)
Five 7"-wide strips, turquoise (space 5)

Borders, Binding

Five 2½"-wide strips, purple (first border)

Six 4½"-wide strips, kid's theme print (second border)

Six 2½"-wide strips, binding fabric

INSTRUCTIONS

Note: *Read How Do I Make the Block?, pages 9 to 14, before beginning.*

1. Using patterns on pages 38 and 39, make 24 foundations each for Block A and Block B, referring to How Do I Make the Foundation?, page 6.

2. Make the block sections using the Cutting Instructions as a guide. (**Diagram 1**)

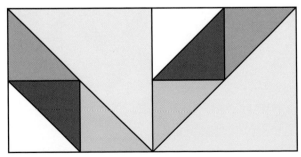

make 24   make 24

Diagram 1

3. For Block A, sew two A sections together noting position; repeat. (**Diagram 2**)

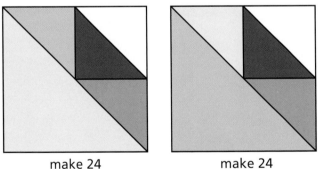

Diagram 2

4. Sew pairs of sections together. Make six blocks. (**Diagram 3**)

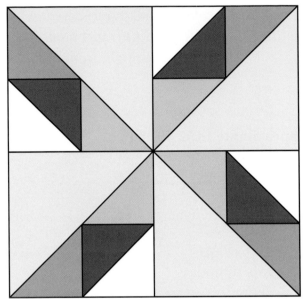

Diagram 3   Block A - make 6

5. Repeat steps 3 and 4 for six Block B using B sections. (**Diagram 4**)

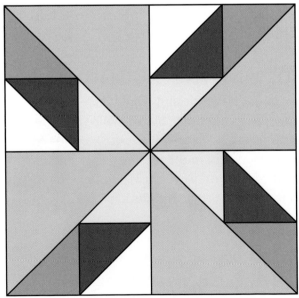

Diagram 4   Block B - make 6

6. Referring to Layout, place blocks in four rows of three blocks alternating Blocks A and B.

7. Sew blocks together in rows. Press seams for rows in alternating directions then sew rows together.

8. Refer to How do I Make a Complete Quilt?, pages 14 to 18, to add borders and finish your quilt.

London's Pinwheels Quilt Layout

LONDON'S PINWHEELS
BLOCK A PATTERN

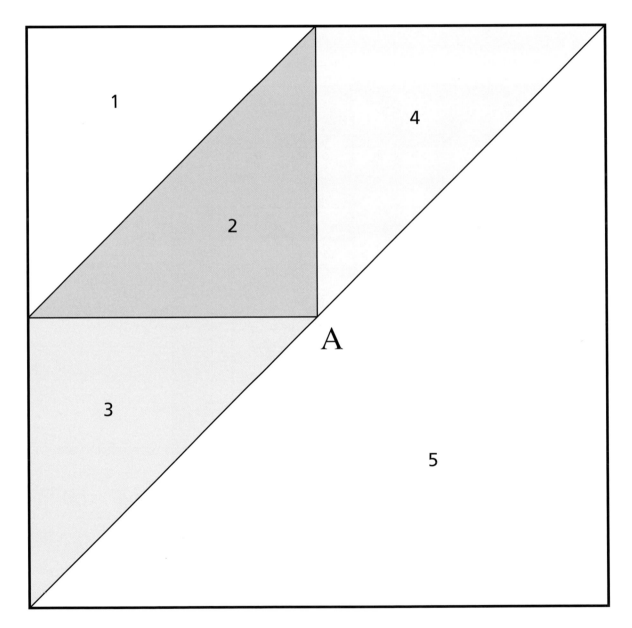

1

2

4

A

3

5

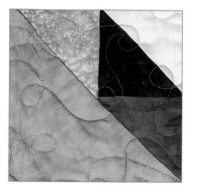

LONDON'S PINWHEELS
BLOCK B PATTERN

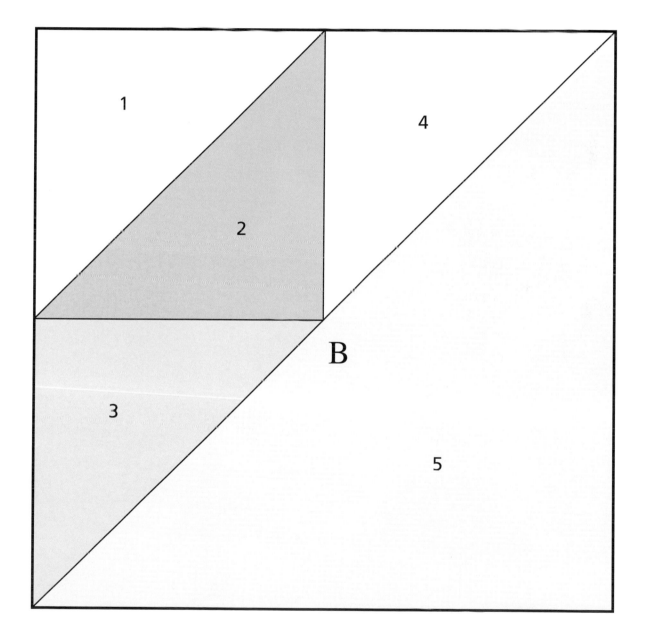

CRAZY QUILT

No book of foundation-pieced quilts would be complete without a Crazy Quilt, which has always used foundation piecing. Keep the quilt simple, or add decorative embroidery stitches by hand or machine. Add trims, laces, charms, and buttons for a quilt that will be cherished for generations.

Approximate Size: 30" x 30"
Block Size: 7" finished
Number of Blocks: 13

MATERIALS

Assorted scraps or fat quarters
1⅛ yds black (includes binding)
1 yds backing fabric
Batting

CUTTING INSTRUCTIONS

For Foundation piecing, you do not have to cut exact pieces. To make it easier for you, however, I have given you the size to cut rectangles for each space. This will make piecing easier and may waste less fabric. You will need 13 assorted rectangles for each of the sizes listed below.

13–3" x 4" rectangles (space 1)
13–3½" x 3" rectangles (space 2)
13–3½" x 5" rectangles (space 3)
13–3" x 6" rectangles (space 4)
13–2¼" x 8" rectangles (space 5)
13–2" x 6" rectangles (space 6)
13–3" x 6½" rectangles (space 7)

Setting Triangles, Binding
Two 12" squares cut into quarters diagonally, black (setting triangles)

Two 7" squares cut in half diagonally, black (corner triangles)
Four 2½"-wide strips, black (binding)

INSTRUCTIONS

Note: Read How Do I Make the Block?, pages 9 to 14, before beginning.

1. Using pattern on page 43, make 13 foundations referring to How Do I Make the Foundation?, page 6.

2. Make blocks using assorted fabrics using Cutting Instructions above as a guide. (**Diagram 1**)

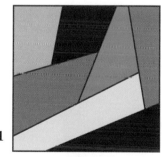

Diagram 1

make 13

3. Referring to Layout on page 42, place blocks in diagonal rows turning blocks in different directions to give a more random look. Place setting triangles at end of each row and corner triangles at each corner.

4. Sew blocks together in diagonal rows. Press seams for rows in alternating directions then sew rows together. (**Diagram 2**)

5. Refer to How Do I Make a Complete Quilt?, pages 14 to 18, to finish quilt. ***Note:*** *Photographed quilt is machine embroidered along each seam.*

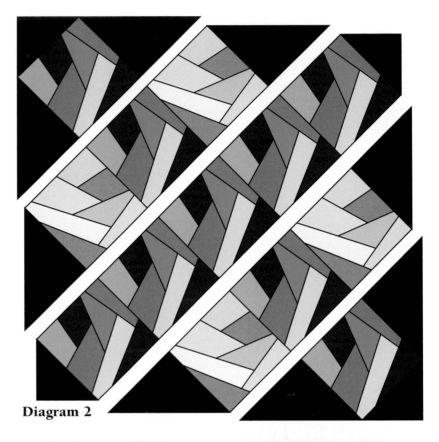

Diagram 2

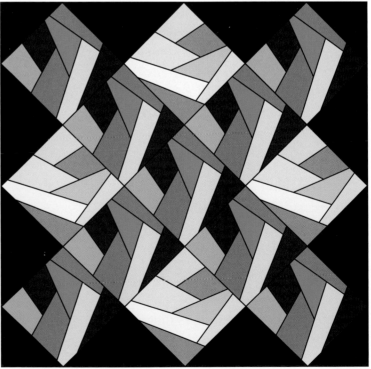

Crazy Quilt Layout

CRAZY QUILT
BLOCK PATTERN

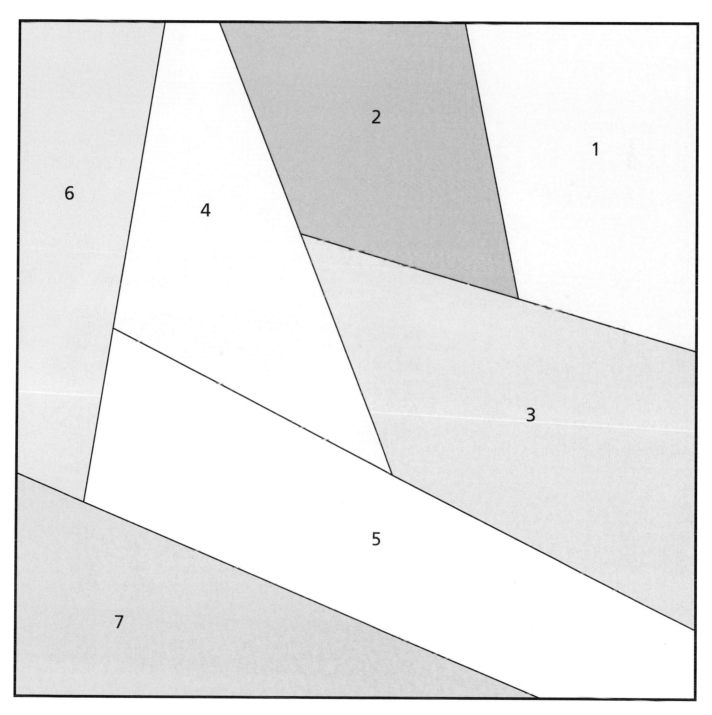

STARBURST

If you attempted to piece this quilt via the traditional method, you would find that meeting all of those triangles in each block an extremely tedious chore. Using the foundation method, however, the quilt blocks go together simply and easily. You'll be proud to display the finished quilt with its dark blue spinning stars that seem to burst as the color fades out to the edges of a second set of green stars.

Approximate Size: 52" x 66"
Block Size: 14" finished
Number of Blocks: 12

MATERIALS

1 yd green
3/4 yd very light pink
3/4 yd light pink
1/2 yd medium pink
1/2 yd medium-dark pink
3/4 yd dark pink
3/4 yd dark blue
1 yd pink floral print
1/2 yd dark blue (first border)
1 yd pink floral (second border)
1/2 yd binding fabric
3 yds backing fabric
Batting

CUTTING INSTRUCTIONS

For Foundation piecing, you do not have to cut exact pieces. To make it easier for you, however, I have given you the size to cut strips for each space. This will make piecing easier and may waste less fabric. If you prefer, follow the instructions on page 7 and cut fabric pieces as you sew.

Ten 2¾"-wide strips, green (space 1)
Ten 2"-wide strips, very light pink (space 2)

Ten 2"-wide strips, light pink (space 3)
Eight 1½"-wide strips, medium pink (space 4)
Eight ½"-wide strips, medium-dark pink (space 5)
Six 3½"-wide strips, dark pink (space 6)
Eleven 2"-wide strips, dark blue (space 7)
24–5" squares (cut in half diagonally), pink floral print (space 8)

45

Borders, Binding

Six 2"-wide strips, dark blue

Seven 4"-wide strips, pink floral print

Seven 2½"-wide strips, binding fabric

INSTRUCTIONS

Note: Read How Do I Make the Block?, pages 9 to 14, before beginning.

1. Using pattern on page 48, prepare 48 foundations referring to How Do I Make the Foundation?, page 6.

2. Make block sections using Cutting Instructions as a guide. (**Diagram 1**)

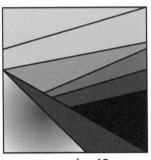

Diagram 1

make 48

3. Sew blocks together in pairs noting position. (**Diagram 2**)

Diagram 2

4. Sew pairs of blocks together to form Starburst block. (**Diagram 3**)

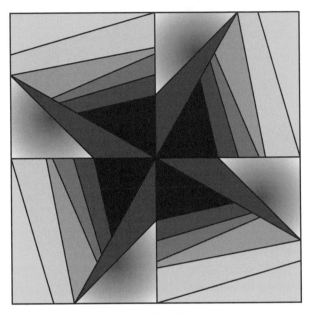

Diagram 3   make 12

5. Repeat steps 2 and 3 for eleven more Starburst blocks.

6. Place the blocks in four rows of three blocks referring to Layout.

7. Sew blocks together in rows. Press seams for rows in opposite directions then sew rows together.

8. Refer to How Do I Make a Complete Quilt?, pages 14 to 18, to add borders and finish your quilt.

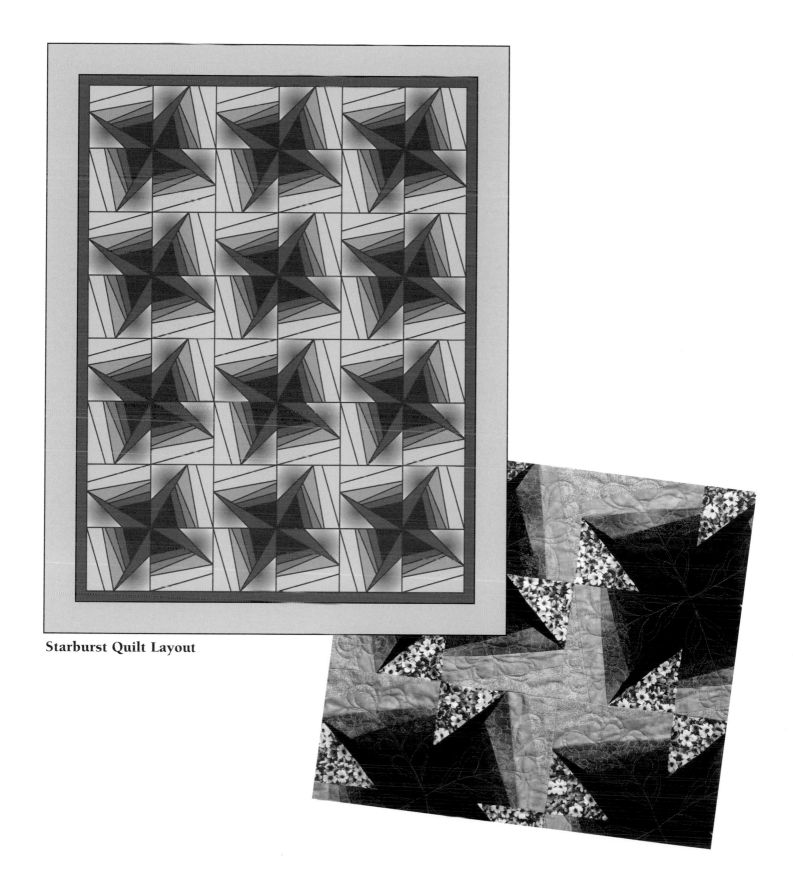

Starburst Quilt Layout

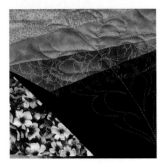

STARBURST
QUARTER-BLOCK PATTERN

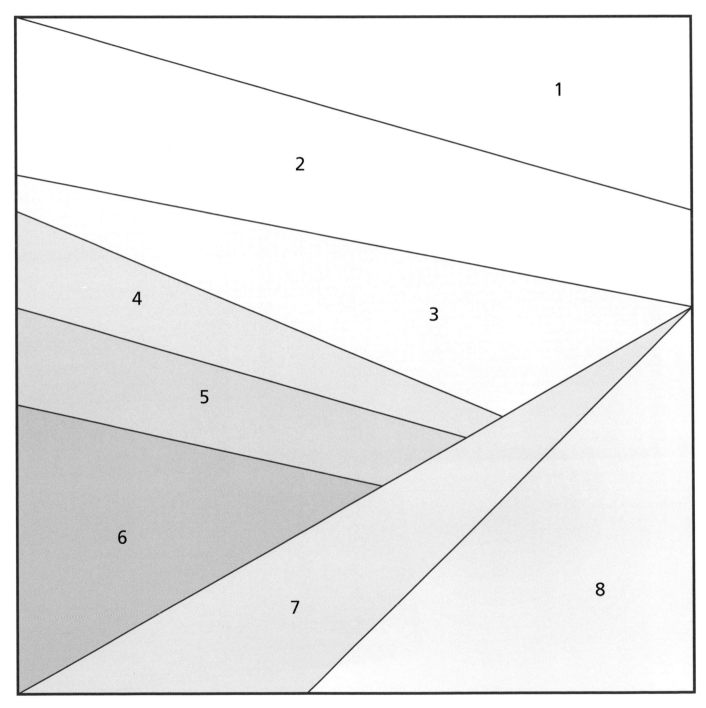

GARDEN PATH

Here is another traditional quilt block made easy by piecing on a foundation. Each block is made up of four smaller foundation sections, which are joined to create the block: a great quilt to make if you are just learning to make foundation pieced blocks with sections. The finished blocks in the quilt form stepping stones with bright pinwheels winding through a garden path of colorful flowers.

Approximate Size: 54" x 70"
Block Size: 8" finished
Number of Blocks: 35

MATERIALS

³/8 yd gold
2⁷/8 yds brown floral print
1⁷/8 yds green print
1 yd coral
2¹/4 yds white
¹/2 yd green print (first border)
1 yd brown floral print (second border)
¹/4 yd coral (flap)
⁵/8 yd binding fabric
3¹/8 yds backing fabric
Batting

CUTTING INSTRUCTIONS

For Foundation piecing, you do not have to cut exact pieces. To make it easier for you, however, I have given you the size to cut strips or squares for each space. This will make piecing easier and may waste less fabric. If you prefer, follow the instructions on page 7 and cut fabric pieces as you sew.

Three 2¹/2"-wide strips each, gold and brown floral (spaces B1 and D1)
Three 3"-wide strips, white (spaces B2, B3 and D2, D3)

35–5" squares (cut in half diagonally) each, green print and brown floral (spaces A3, C3 and B4, D4)
Six 3¹/2"-wide strips, white (spaces A1, C1)
Six 3¹/2"-wide strips, coral (spaces A2, C2)

Borders, Binding
Five 2¹/2"-wide strips, green print (first border)
Six 5¹/2"-wide strips, brown floral print (second border)
Six 1"-wide strips, coral (flap)
Seven 2¹/2"-wide strips, binding fabric

INSTRUCTIONS

Note: *Read How Do I Make the Block?, pages 9 to 14, before beginning.*

1. Using the pattern on page 53, prepare 35 foundations of each section: A, B, C, D referring to How Do I Make the Foundation?, page 6.

2. Sew all sections using the Cutting Instructions as a guide. (**Diagram 1**)

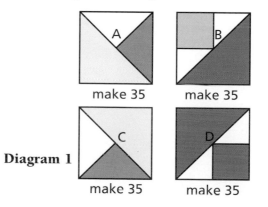

Diagram 1

A make 35
B make 35
C make 35
D make 35

3. Sew a Section A to a Section B noting position. Repeat for remaining A and B. (**Diagram 2**)

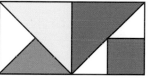

Diagram 2

4. Sew each Section C to a Section D noting position. Repeat for remaining C and D. (**Diagram 3**)

Diagram 3

5. Sew pairs of sections together to complete block. (**Diagram 4**)

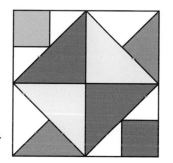

Diagram 4

6. Place blocks in seven rows of five blocks referring to Layout on page 52.

7. For first border, measure length of quilt; cut and sew green border strips to sides. Measure quilt crosswise; cut strips, then sew to top and bottom.

8. For the flap and second border, measure length of quilt then piece and cut two 1"-wide coral strips and two 5½"-wide brown floral print strips to that length. Fold coral strips in half lengthwise with wrong sides together. Place along sides of quilt with raw edges even; pin in place. (**Diagram 5**)

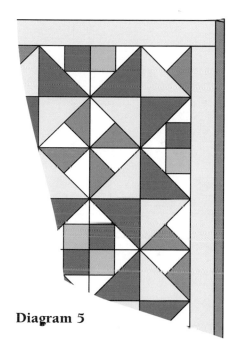

Diagram 5

9. Place 5½"-wide brown floral print strips on sides of quilt. Folded coral strip will be sandwiched between green and brown floral print strips. Sew in place. Press border strip open, being sure seam allowance is toward brown floral strip. **Note:** *This pressing is important so that flap lies in correct position.*

10. Measure quilt crosswise, then repeat steps 8 and 9 for top and bottom flap and brown floral print border.

11. Finish quilt referring to How Do I Make a Complete Quilt?, pages 14 to 18.

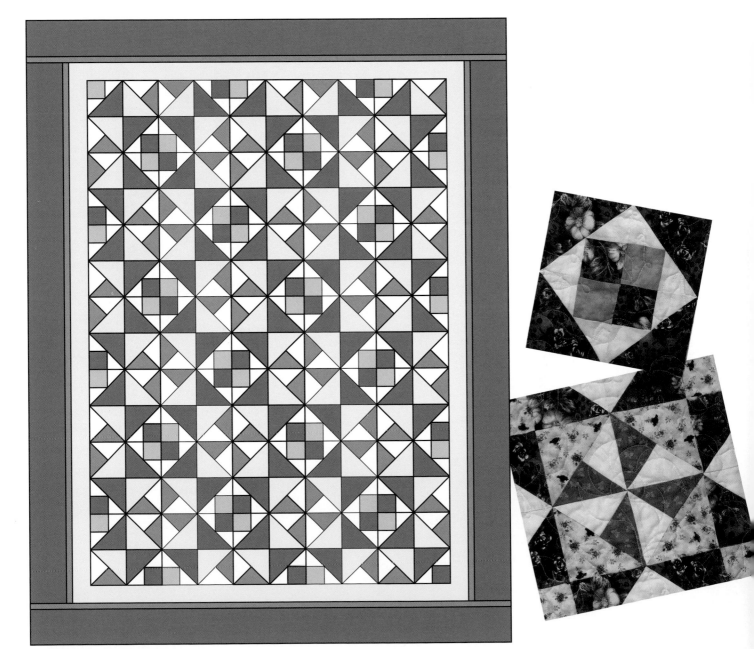

Garden Path Quilt Layout

GARDEN PATH
BLOCK PATTERN

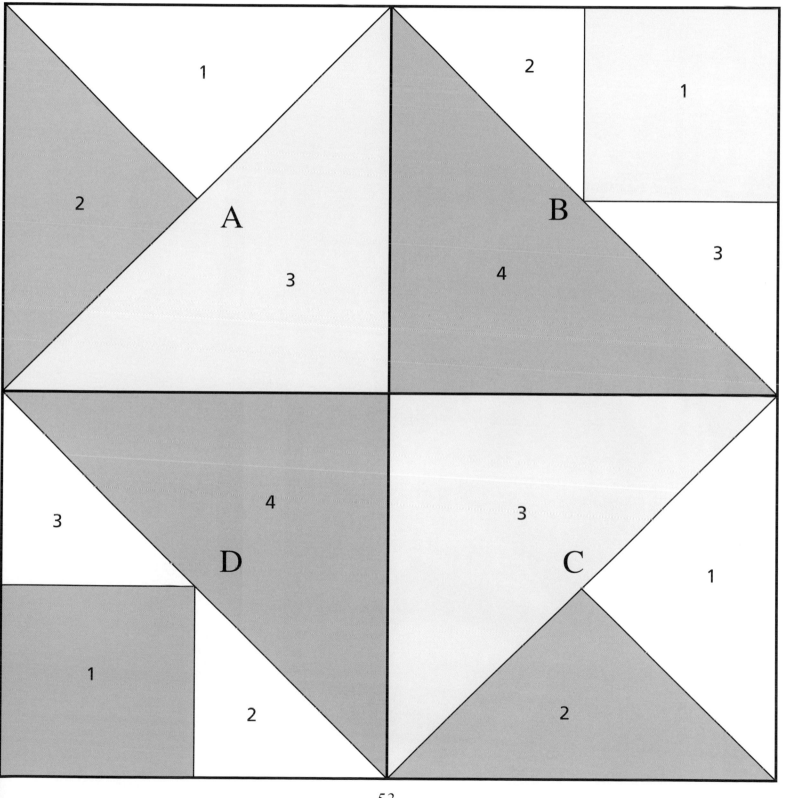

STARS AND DIAMONDS

This complex-lookng quilt is made up of a single, simple block. Placing the blocks in a diagonal setting forms stars surrounded by diamonds. Changing the color of the first space in some of the blocks from white to dark blue, frames this quilt in dramatic fashion.

Approximate Size: 45½" x 45½"
Block Size: 7" finished
Number of Blocks: 16 A blocks,
  20 B blocks, 4 C blocks

MATERIALS

1 yd very light blue
¼ yd blue/purple specks
⅝ yd light blue
⅝ yd medium-light blue
⅞ yd medium blue
1½ yds dark purple
¾ yd dark blue
½ yd binding fabric
2¼ yds backing fabric
Batting

CUTTING INSTRUCTIONS

For Foundation piecing, you do not have to cut exact pieces. To make it easier for you, however, I have given you the size to cut strips for each space. This will make piecing easier and may waste less fabric. If you prefer, follow the instructions on page 7 and cut fabric pieces as you sew.

Five 4¼"-wide strips, medium-light blue (space A1)
Six 4¼"-wide strips, very light blue (space B1)
One 4¼"-wide strips, blue/purple specks (space C1)

18–2¼"-wide strips, dark purple (spaces 2, 5)
11–1¼"-wide strips, medium blue (spaces 3, 6)
Eight 2"-wide strips, light blue (spaces 4, 7)

Borders, Binding
Three 11" squares cut in quarters diagonally, dark blue (setting triangles)
Two 11" squares cut in half diagonally, dark blue (corner triangles)
Six 2½"-wide strips, binding fabric

55

INSTRUCTIONS

Note: *Read How Do I Make the Block?, pages 9 to 14, before beginning.*

1. Using patterns on pages 58 to 60, make 16 Block A, 20 Block B, and four Block C foundations referring to How Do I Make the Foundation?, page 6.

2. Make 16 Block A, 20 Block B and four Block C using Cutting Instructions as a guide. (**Diagram 1**)

3. Place blocks in diagonal rows. (**Diagram 2**)

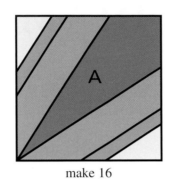
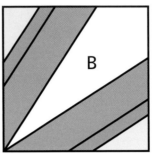
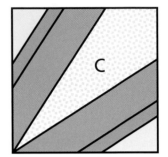

make 16   make 20   make 4

Diagram 1

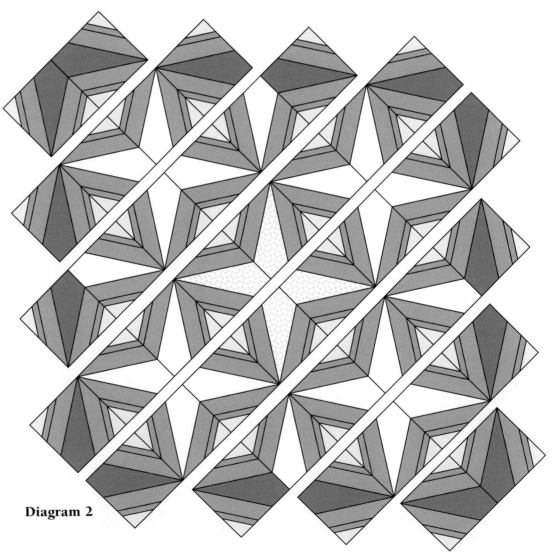

Diagram 2

56

4. Place setting triangles at ends of rows and a corner triangle in each corner referring to Layout.

5. Sew blocks together in rows. Press seams for rows in opposite directions then sew rows together. Add corner triangles last.

6. Trim edges of quilt top even ¼" from outer corner of blocks.

7. Refer to How Do I Make a Complete Quilt?, pages 14 to 18, to finish quilt.

Stars and Diamonds Quilt Layout

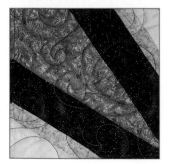

STARS AND DIAMONDS
BLOCK A PATTERN

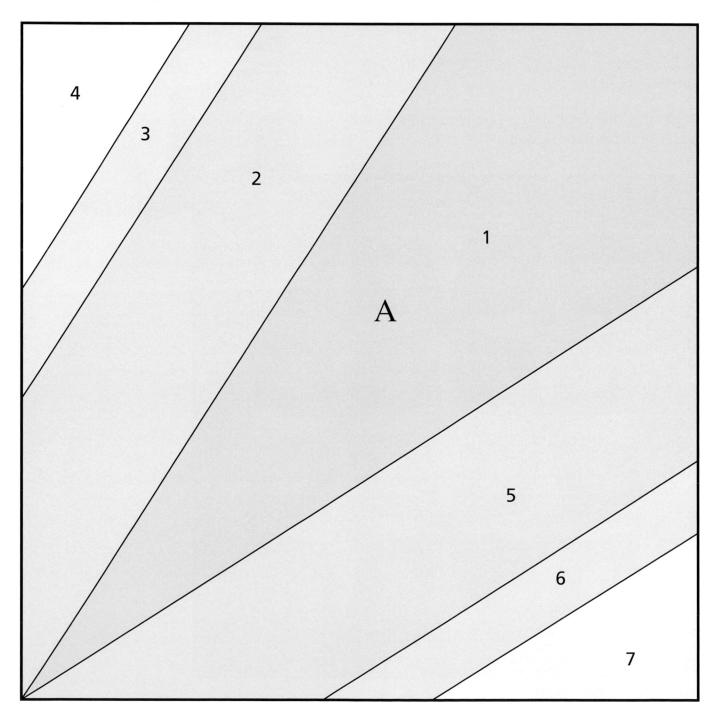

STARS AND DIAMONDS
BLOCK B PATTERN

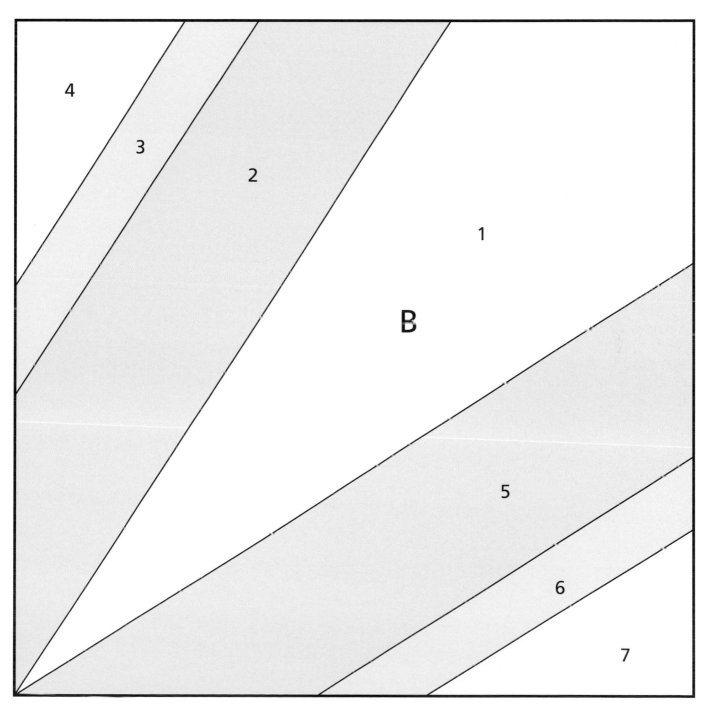

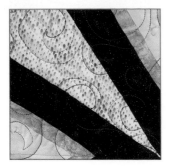

STARS AND DIAMONDS
BLOCK C PATTERN

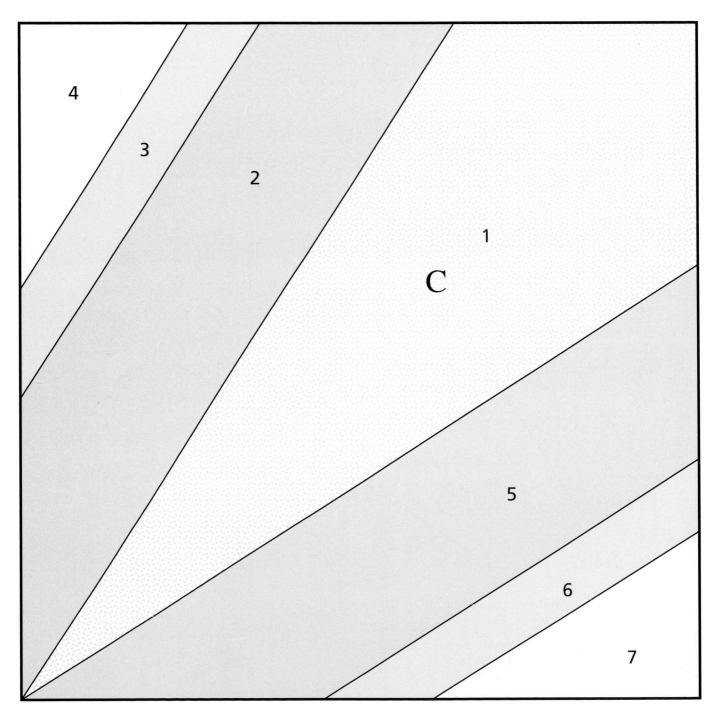

NIGHT STARS

Eight triangular sections are each foundation pieced and then joined together to create the block. The black fabric is a stunning background for the vibrant stars that march across the quilt. This simple—but dramatic—quilt was made using only two fabrics: black and a multi-colored print by FreeSpirit®.

Approximate Size: 46" x 60"
Block Size: 14" finished
Number of Blocks: 12

MATERIALS

3 yards multi-color
2¹/₂ yards black (includes border)
¹/₂ yd binding fabric
3 yds backing fabric
Batting

CUTTING INSTRUCTIONS

For Foundation piecing, you do not have to cut exact pieces. To make it easier for you, however, I have given you the size to cut strips for each space. This will make piecing easier and may waste less fabric. If you prefer, follow the instructions on page 7 and cut fabric pieces as you sew.

19–3¹/₂"-wide strips, black (space A1, B1)
16–2³/₄"-wide strips, multi (space A2, B2)
13–3¹/₂"-wide strips, multi (space A3, B3)

Borders, Binding

Six 2¹/₂"-wide strips, black (border)
Six 2¹/₂"-wide strips, binding fabric

INSTRUCTIONS

Note: *Read How Do I Make the Block?, pages 9 to 14, before beginning.*

1. Using pattern on page 65, make 48 foundations referring to How Do I Make the Foundation?, page 6.

2. Make 48 of each triangle A and B using the Cutting Instructions as a guide. (**Diagram 1**)

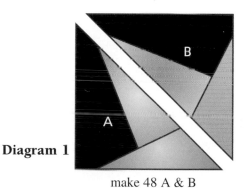

Diagram 1

make 48 A & B

3. Sew triangles A and B together to complete a quarter square. Make 47 more squares. (**Diagram 2**)

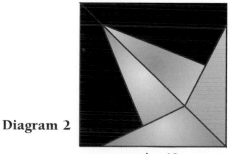

Diagram 2

make 48

4. Sew two quarter blocks together; repeat. (**Diagram 3**)

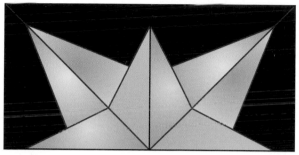

Diagram 3

5. Sew pairs of quarter blocks together to complete Star Block. (**Diagram 4**)

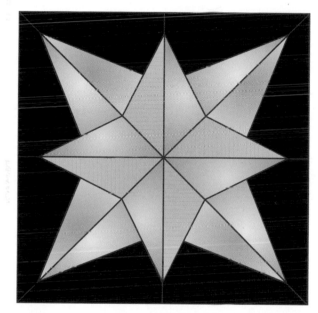

Diagram 4   make 12

6. Repeat steps 4 and 5 for eleven more blocks.

7. Place blocks in four rows of three blocks referring to Layout on page 64.

8. Sew blocks together in rows. Press seams for rows in alternating directions then sew rows together.

9. Refer to How Do I Make a Complete Quilt?, pages 14 to 18 to add border and finish quilt.

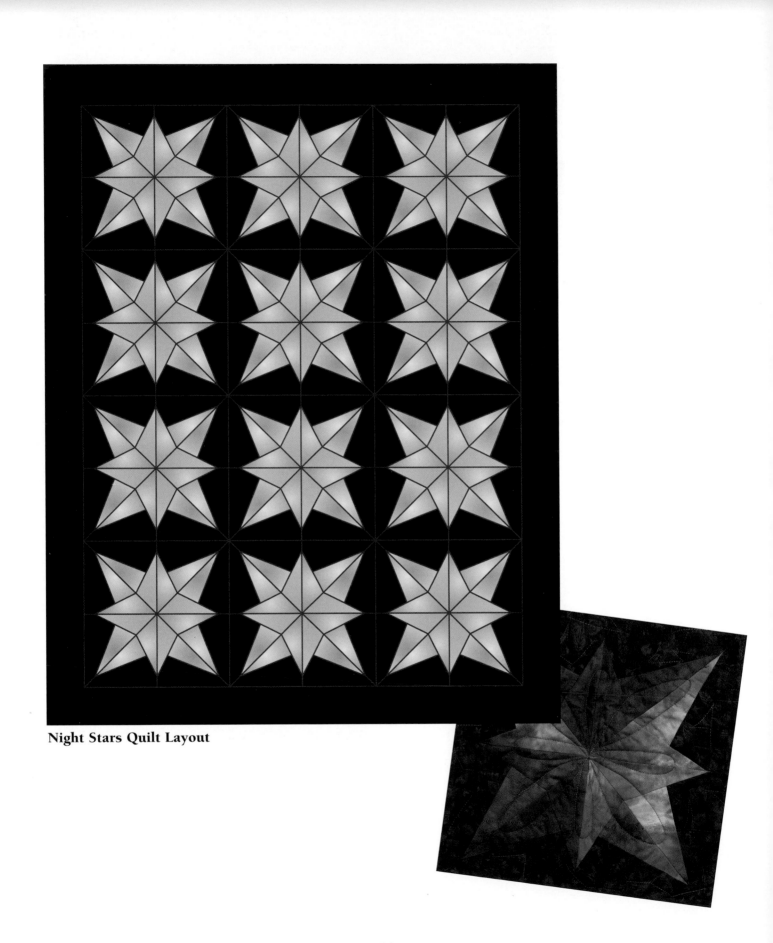

Night Stars Quilt Layout

NIGHT STARS
QUARTER-BLOCK PATTERN

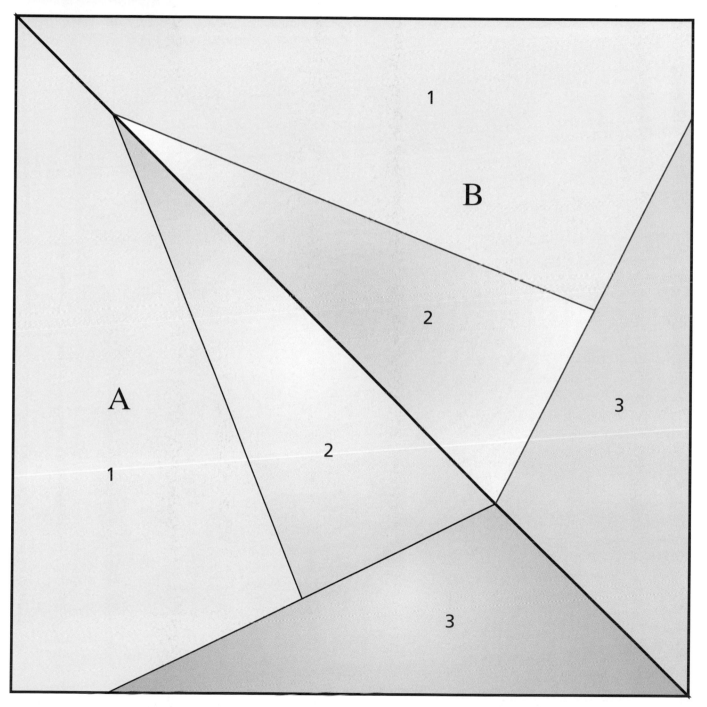

DIAMONDS AND SQUARES

A quilted wall hanging that is simple to make and dramatic to look at: two rectangles are pieced and then joined to create the square. There are no circles in the pattern, and yet, after the quilt is pieced clusters of rosebuds alternate with diamonds and form circles that seem to overlap.

Approximate Size: 49" x 49"
Block Size: 7" finished
Number of Blocks: 36

MATERIALS

1¼ yards light blue
½ yard dark blue
¾ yard dark green
½ yard floral print
½ yrd burgundy
¾ yard floral print (border)
½ yd binding fabric
3 yds backing fabric
Batting

CUTTING INSTRUCTIONS

For Foundation piecing, you do not have to cut exact pieces. To make it easier for you, however, I have given you the size to cut strips for each space. This will make piecing easier and may waste less fabric. If you prefer, follow the instructions on page 7 and cut fabric pieces as you sew.

Block 1

One 3"-wide strip, light blue (space A1)
Two 2¼"-wide strips, dark blue (space A2, A3, B4)
One 2¼"-wide strip, burgundy (spaces A4, B5)
Two 4½" squares (cut in half diagonally), floral print (space B1)

Two 4½" squares (cut in half diagonally), burgundy (space B2)
One 2¼"-wide strip, light blue (space B3)

Block II

Four 3"-wide strips, light blue (space A1)
Seven 2¼"-wide strips, dark green (spaces A2, A3, B4)
Four 2¼"-wide strips, burgundy (spaces A4, B5)
Eight 4½" squares (cut in half diagonally), floral print (space B1)
Eight 4½" squares (cut in half diagonally), burgundy (space B2)
Two 2¼"-wide strips, light blue (space B3)

Block III

Two 3"-wide strips, light blue (space A1)
Two 2¼"-wide strips, dark green (spaces A2, B4)
Two 2¼"-wide strips, dark blue (space A 3)
Two 2¼"-wide strips, burgundy (spaces A4, B5)
Four 4½" squares (cut in half diagonally), floral print (space B1)
Four 4½" squares (cut in half diagonally), burgundy (space B2)
One 2¼"-wide strip, light blue (space B3)

Block IV

Two 3"-wide strips, light blue (space A1)
Two 2¼"-wide strips, dark blue (space A2, B4)
Two 2¼"-wide strips, dark green (space A3)
Two 2¼"-wide strips, burgundy (space A4, B5)

Four 4½"-wide squares (cut in half diagonally), floral print (space B1)

Four 4½" squares (cut in half diagonally), burgundy (space B2)

One 2¼" strip, light blue (space B3)

Borders, Binding

Six 4"-wide strips, floral print

Six 2½"-wide strips, binding fabric

INSTRUCTIONS

Note: *Read How Do I Make the Block?, pages 9 to 14, before beginning.*

1. Using patterns on pages 70 to 73, make foundations for four Block I, 16 Block II, eight Block III and eight Block IV referring to How Do I Make the Foundation?, page 6.

2. Make sections A and B for all blocks referring to Cutting Instructions as a guide. (**Diagram 1**)

Block I
make 4 A and B

Block II
make 16 A and B

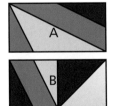
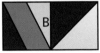

Block III
make 8 A and B

Block IV
make 8 A and B

Diagram 1

3. Sew sections A and B together to make four Block I, 16 Block II, eight Block III and eight Block IV. (**Diagram 2**)

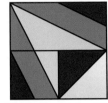

Block I - make 4   Block II - make 16

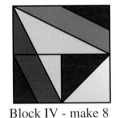

Block III - make 8   Block IV - make 8

Diagram 2

4. Place blocks in six rows of six blocks referring to Layout on page 69. Note that dark blue is along outer edges of quilt top.

5. Sew blocks together in rows. Press seams for rows in opposite directions then sew rows together.

6. Refer to How Do I Make a Complete Quilt?, pages 14 to 18, to add border and finish quilt.

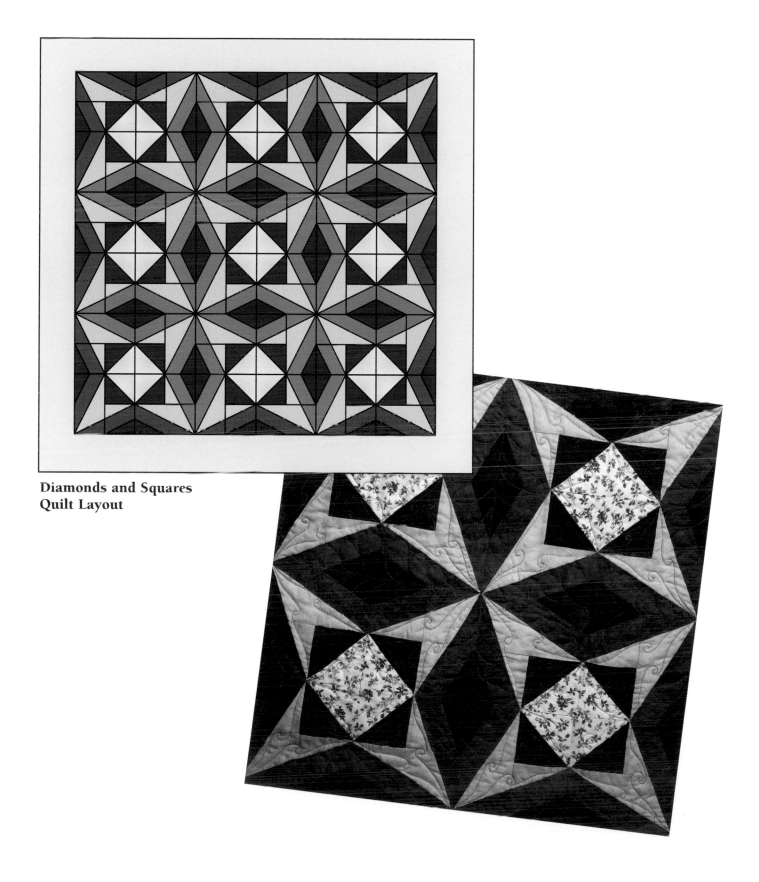

**Diamonds and Squares
Quilt Layout**

DIAMONDS AND SQUARES
BLOCK I PATTERN

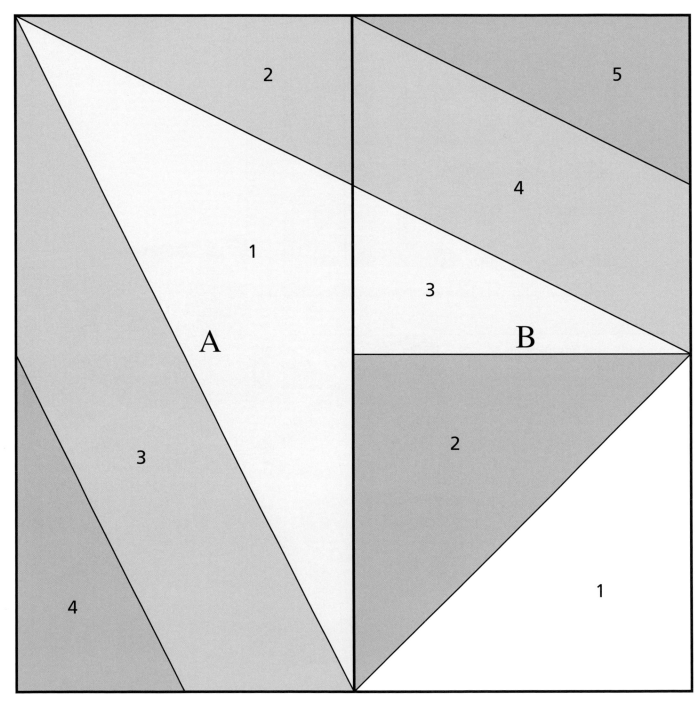

DIAMONDS AND SQUARES
BLOCK II PATTERN

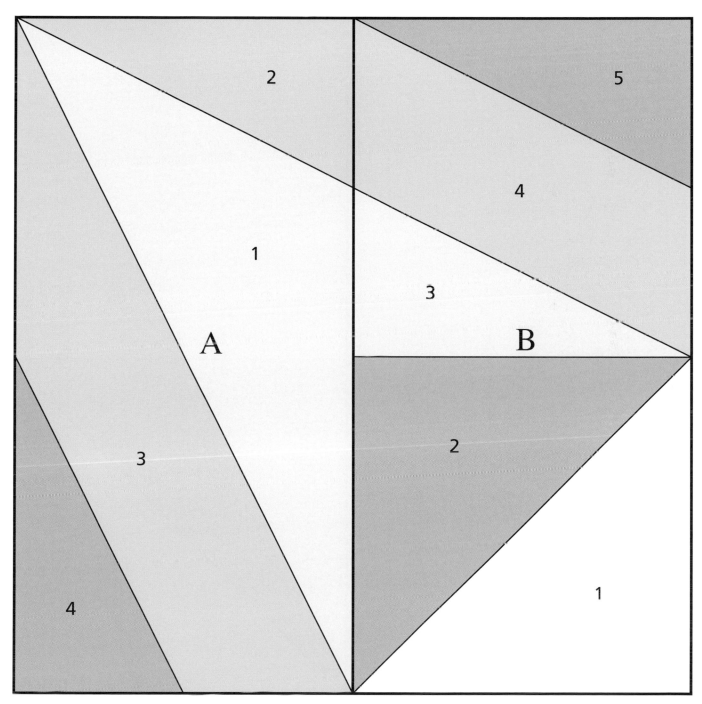

2

5

1

4

3

A

B

3

2

4

1

71

DIAMONDS AND SQUARES
BLOCK III PATTERN

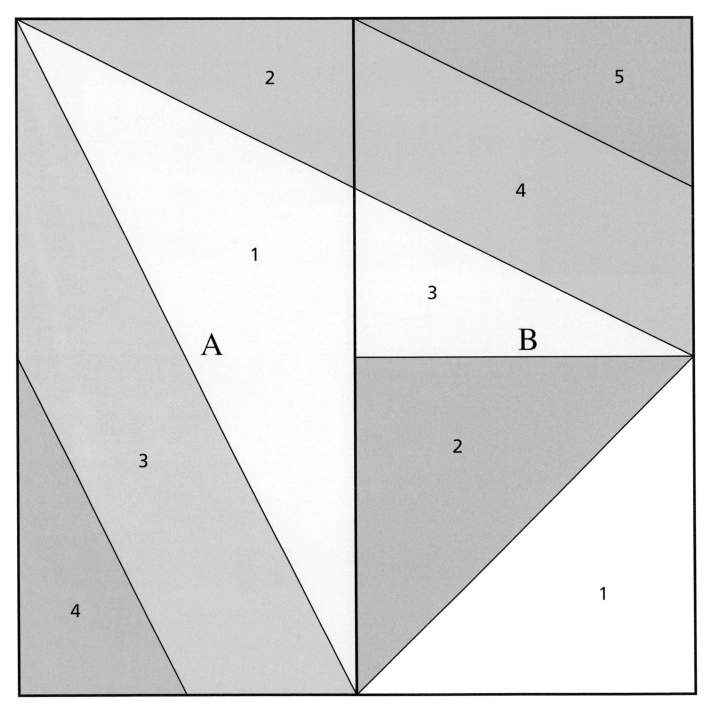

DIAMONDS AND SQUARES
BLOCK IV PATTERN

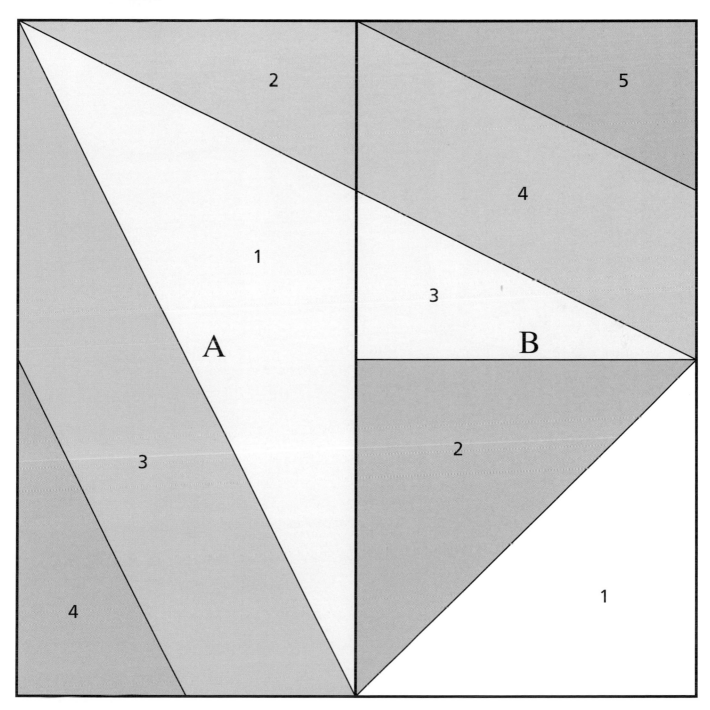

FRAMED STARS

Only the most experienced quilter would attempt to make this quilt using traditional templates.
Using the foundation method, however, this is a quilt even a rank beginner can complete.
The striped circles act as frames for the brightly-colored stars that seem to spring from
the surface of the quilt.

Approximate Size: 57" x 57"
Block Size: 15" finished
Number of Blocks: 9

MATERIALS

1¼ yards very light aqua
1¼ yards light peach
1¼ yards medium peach
½ yard dark peach
¾ yard light aqua
¾ yard medium aqua
½ yard dark aqua
⅜ yard dark peach (first border)
⅜ yard light aqua (second border)
¾ yard dark aqua (third border)
¾ yard binding fabric
3½ yards backing fabric
Batting

CUTTING INSTRUCTIONS

For Foundation piecing, you do not have to cut exact pieces. To make it easier for you, however, I have given you the size to cut strips for each space. This will make piecing easier and may waste less fabric. If you prefer, follow the instructions on page 7 and cut fabric pieces as you sew.

Eight 2¼"-wide strips, very light aqua (space A1)
Six 1"-wide strips, dark peach (space A2)
Four 1¼"-wide strips, dark aqua (space A3)
Seven 2¾"-wide strips, medium aqua (space A4)
Eight 4½"-wide strips, medium peach (space A5)
Eight 2¼"-wide strips, very light aqua (space B1)
Six 1"-wide strips, dark peach (space B2)
Four 1¼"-wide strips, dark aqua (space B3)
Seven 2¾"-wide strips, light aqua (space B4)
Eight 4½"-wide strips, light peach (space B5)

Borders, Binding

Five 2"-wide strips, dark peach (first border)
Six 1½"-wide sttips, light aqua (second border)
Six 4"-wide strips, dark aqua (third border)
Six 2½"-wide strips, binding fabric

INSTRUCTIONS

Note: *Read How Do I Make the Block?, pages 9 to 14, before beginning.*

1. Using patterns on page 78, make 48 foundations of each triangle referring to How Do I Make the Foundation?, page 6.

2. Make all triangles using the Cutting Instructions as a guide. (**Diagram 1**)

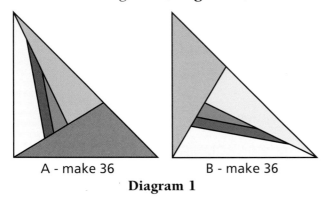

A - make 36   B - make 36

Diagram 1

3. Sew a triangle A to a triangle B for a quarter square; repeat for a total of 48 quarter blocks. (**Diagram 2**)

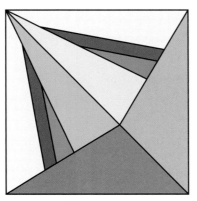

Diagram 2

4. Sew two quarter blocks together; repeat. (**Diagram 3**)

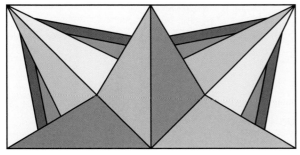

Diagram 3

5. Sew pairs of quarter blocks together to complete block. Make eight more blocks (**Diagram 4**)

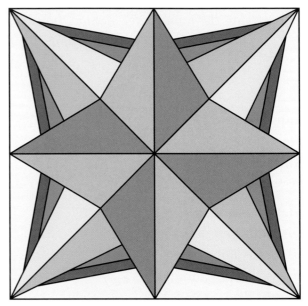

Diagram 4

76

6. Referring to Layout, place blocks in four rows of three blocks.

7. Sew blocks together in rows. Press seams for rows in alternating directions then sew rows together.

8. Refer to How Do I Make a Complete Quilt?, pages 14 to 18, to add borders and finish quilt.

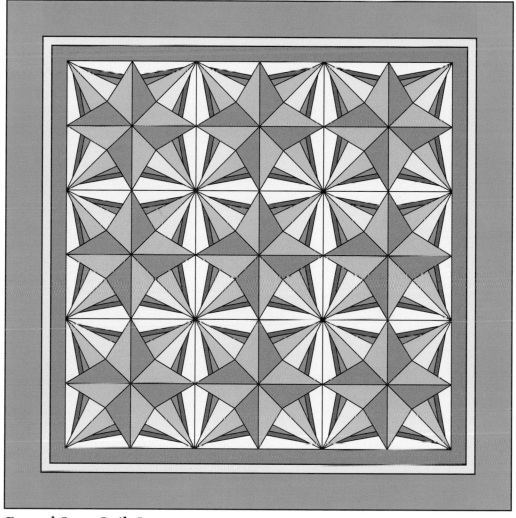

Framed Stars Quilt Layout

77

FRAMED STARS
QUARTER-BLOCK PATTERN

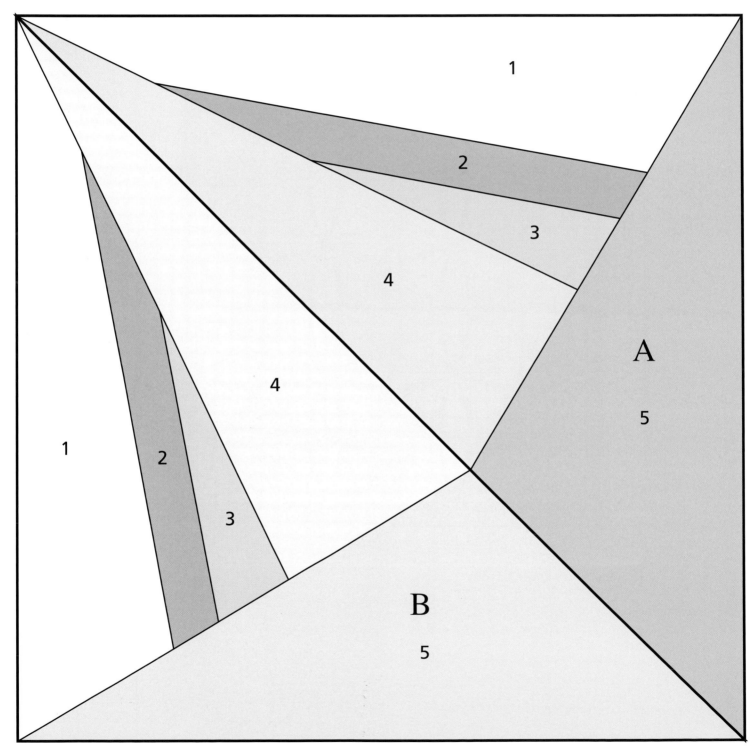

SPIDER WEB STARS

Imagine the careful piecing that would be required to complete the quilt if you chose to make it with templates! With the foundation-piecing method, it can be completed in no time. The blocks give the impression of stars created by spider webs, and the fabrics used in this quilt truly add to the spider web effect. Look closely and you will see an "X" and a diamond intersect across this lively quilt.

Approximate Size: 51" x 51"
Block Size: 14" finished
Number of Blocks: 5 Block A and 4 Block B

MATERIALS

1 yd blue multi print (includes second border)
1 yd turquoise multi print (includes second border)
3/4 yd purple
1/2 yd peach multi print
3/8 yd pink multi print
3/8 yd purple multi print
3/8 yd orange multi print
1/2 yd purple (first border)
1/2 yd binding fabric
2 1/2 yds backing fabric
Batting

CUTTING INSTRUCTIONS

For Foundation piecing, you do not have to cut exact pieces. To make it easier for you, however, I have given you the size to cut strips for each space. This will make piecing easier and may waste less fabric. If you prefer, follow the instructions on page 7 and cut fabric pieces as you sew.

Four 3 1/2"-wide strips, blue multi print (space A1)
Two 3 1/2"-wide strips, turquoise multi print (space B1)

Eight 1 1/4"-wide strips, purple (spaces 2, 4, 6, 8)
Five 1 3/4"-wide strips, peach multi print (spaces 3, 7)
Seven 2 3/4"-wide strips, pink multi print (space 9)
Seven 2 3/4"-wide strips, purple multi print (space 5)
Two 3 1/4"-wide strips, orange multi print (space 10)

Borders, Binding
Five 1 1/4"-wide strips, purple (first border)
Two 4 1/4"-wide strips, turquoise multi print (second border)

Two 4¼"-wide strips, blue multi print
(second border)

Four 4¼" squares, pink multi print
(cornerstones)

Six 2½"-wide strips, binding fabric

INSTRUCTIONS

Note: *Read How Do I Make the Block?, pages 9 to 14, before beginning.*

1. Using patterns A and B on pages 83 and 84, make foundations for 40 A Triangles and 32 B Triangles referring to How Do I Make the Foundation?, page 6.

2. Make all A and B Triangle blocks using Cutting Instructions as a guide. (**Diagram 1**)

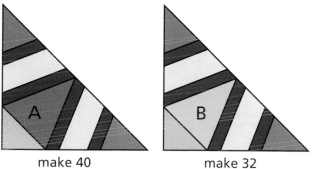

make 40   make 32

Diagram 1

3. Sew two A Triangle blocks together to form a square. (**Diagram 2**) Repeat for 19 more A Squares.

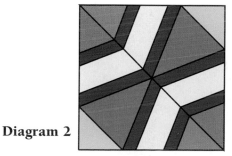

Diagram 2

make 20

4. Sew two B Triangle blocks together to form a square. (**Diagram 3**) Repeat for 15 more B Squares.

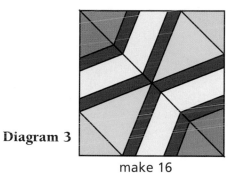

Diagram 3

make 16

5. Sew four A squares together to form a Spider Web Star A. (**Diagram 4**) Repeat for four more blocks.

Diagram 4   make 5

6. Sew four B Squares together to form Spider Web Star B. (**Diagram 5**) Repeat for three more blocks.

Diagram 5   make 4

7. Place blocks in three rows of three, alternating A and B blocks referring to Layout.

8. Sew blocks together in rows. Press seams for rows in opposite directions then sew rows together.

9. Refer to How Do I Make a Complete Quilt?, pages 14 to 18, to add borders and finish your quilt. *Note: For second border, sew blue multi print border strips to sides of quilt top. Sew a pink multi print square to each end of turquoise multi print strips; sew to top and bottom of quilt.*

**Spider Web Stars
Quilt Layout**

SPIDER WEB STARS
QUARTER-BLOCK A PATTERN

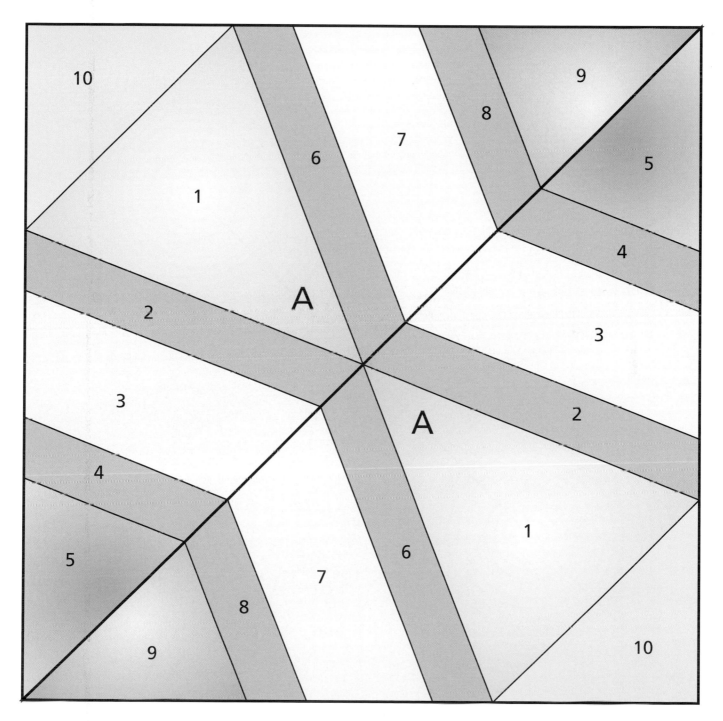

SPIDER WEB STARS
QUARTER-BLOCK B PATTERN

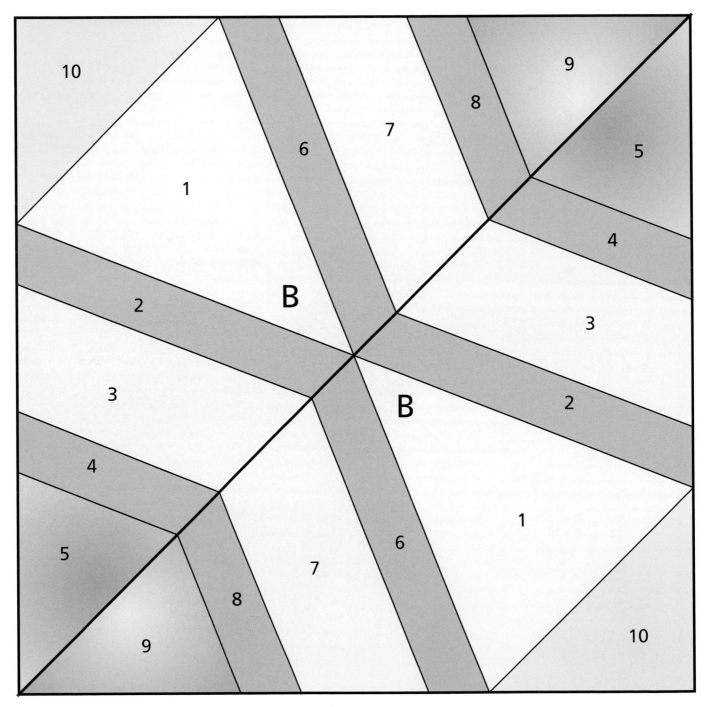

PATRIOTIC HOLIDAY

Two sizes of the old favorite quilt pattern, "Flying Geese," take off on a patriotic holiday through a maze of blue and red fabrics. Because this little wall hanging can be finished so quickly, you might want to make it in a variety of colors for every holiday in the calendar.

Approximate Size: 24" x 24"
Block Size: 6" finished
Number of Blocks: 9

MATERIALS

1/2 yard light blue
3/8 yard dark blue
1/2 yard medium red
3/8 yard dark red
1/4 yard light blue (first border)
1 1/8 yards dark blue (second border)
1/4 yard binding fabric
3/4 yard backing fabric
Batting

CUTTING INSTRUCTIONS

For Foundation piecing, you do not have to cut exact pieces. To make it easier for you, however, I have given you the size to cut strips for each space. This will make piecing easier and may waste less fabric. If you prefer, follow the instructions on page 7 and cut out fabric pieces as you sew.

Two 1 1/4"-wide strips, dark red (space 1)
Six 1 3/4"-wide strips, light blue (spaces 2, 3, 5, 6)
Two 1 1/4"-wide strips, dark blue (space 4)

Two 2 1/2"-wide strips, dark red (space 7)
Two 2 1/2"-wide strips, medium red (space 8)
Four 2"-wide strips, dark blue (space 9)
Four 2 1/2"-wide strips, medium red (spaces 10, 11)

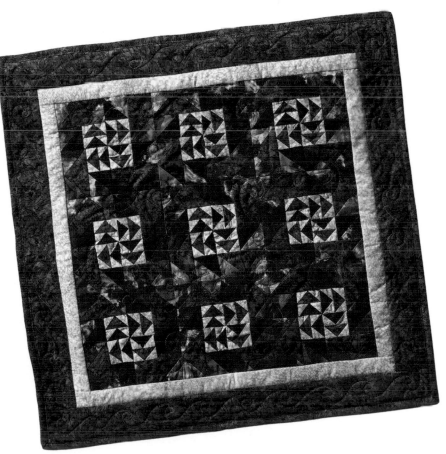

Borders, Binding

Two 1½"-wide strips, light blue (first border)

Three 2½"-wide strips, dark blue (second border)

Three 2½"-wide strips, binding fabric

INSTRUCTIONS

Note: Read How Do I Make the Block?, pages 9 to 14, before beginning.

1. Using pattern on page 89, make nine foundations referring to How Do I Make the Foundation?, page 6. Cut foundations into four sections.

2. Make the block sections using the Cutting Instructions as a guide. (**Diagram 1**)

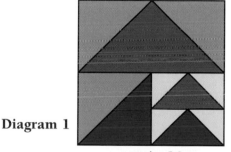

Diagram 1

make 36

3. Sew two block sections together noting placement; repeat. (**Diagram 2**)

Diagram 2

4. Sew pairs of sections together to complete block. (**Diagram 3**)

Diagram 3   make 9

5. Repeat steps 3 to 4 for eight more blocks.

6. Place blocks in three rows of three blocks referring to Layout on page 88.

7. Sew blocks together in rows. Press seams for rows in alternating directions then sew rows together.

8. Refer to How Do I Make a Complete Quilt?, pages 14 to 18, to add borders and finish your quilt.

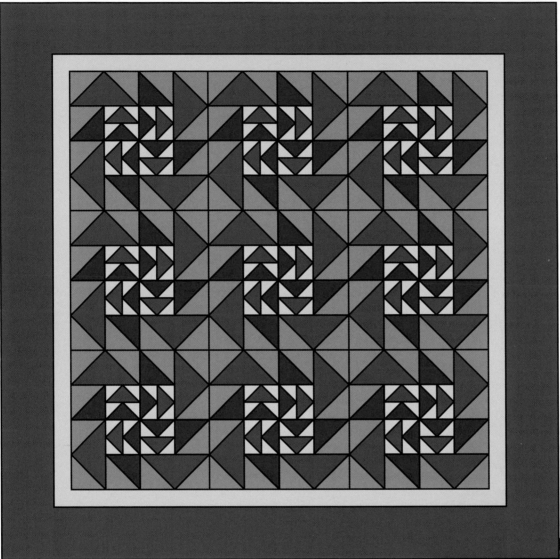

Patriotic Holiday Quilt Layout

PATRIOTIC HOLIDAY
BLOCK PATTERN

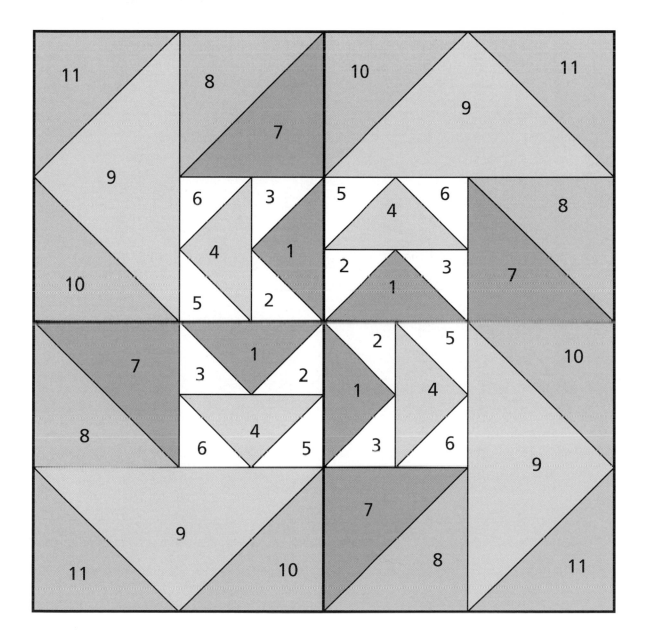

QUILTER'S GIFT

There are five easy-to-piece foundation sections in each block, allowing the little quilt to be finished in no time. Make one as a gift for your favorite quilter by using quilter's novelty prints. It will make the perfect addition to any sewing room. Or, you may wish to use this block and your favorite novelty fabric to personalize a quilt for a special someone.

Approximate Size: 38" x 38"
Block Size: 7" finished
Number of Blocks: 16

MATERIALS

5/8 yard quilter's novelty print

3/8 yard gold print

3/8 yard dark blue print

5/8 yard medium blue fabric

5/8 yard medium beige

5/8 yard light beige print

1 yard medium beige print

5/8 yard very light beige

3/8 yard red print

3/8 yard green print

3/8 yd border 1 print

5/8 yd border 2 print

3/8 yd binding fabric

1 yd backing fabric

Batting

CUTTING INSTRUCTIONS

For Foundation piecing, you do not have to cut exact pieces. To make it easier for you, however, I have given you the size to cut strips for each space. This will make piecing easier and may waste less fabric. If you prefer, follow the instructions on page 7 and cut fabric pieces as you sew.

Block I

Two 4"-wide strips, quilter's novelty print (space A1)

Three 2¾"-wide strips, green print (spaces A2, A3, A4, A5)

Three 1¾"-wide strips, red print (spaces B1)

Seven 1¾"-wide strips, medium beige print (spaces B2, B3, B4)

Three 2¾"-wide strips, very light beige (spaces B5, B6)

Three 1¾"- wide strips, red print (space C1)

Seven 1¾"-wide strips, medium beige print (spaces C2, C3, C4)

Three 2¾"-wide strips, very light beige (spaces C5, C6)

Three 2¾"-wide strips, medium blue print (spaces C7, C8)

Three 2¾"-wide strips, light beige print (spaces C9, C10)

Block II

Two 4"-wide strips, quilter's novelty print (space A1)

Three 2¾"-wide strips, gold print (spaces A2, A3, A4, A5)

Three 1¾"-wide strips, dark blue print (spaces B1)

Seven 1¾"-wide strips, medium beige print (spaces B2, B3, B4)

Three 2¾"-wide strips, very light beige (spaces B5, B6)

Three 1¾"- wide strips, dark blue print (space C1)

Seven 1¾"-wide strips, medium beige print (spaces C2, C3, C4)

Three 2¾"-wide strips, medium beige (spaces C5, C6)

Three 2¾"-wide strips, medium blue print (spaces C7, C8)

Three 2¾"-wide strips, light beige print (spaces C9, C10)

Borders, Binding

Four 2"-wide strips, medium blue (first border)

Four 4"-wide strips, quilter's novelty print (second border)

Four 2¾"-wide strips, binding fabric

INSTRUCTIONS

Note: Read How Do I Make the Block?, pages 9 to 14, before beginning.

1. Using patterns on pages 94 and 95, make eight foundations for Block A and eight foundations for Block B referring to How Do I Make the Foundation?, page 6.

2. Make all block sections using Cutting Instructions as a guide. (**Diagram 1**)

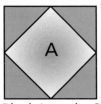
Block I - make 8

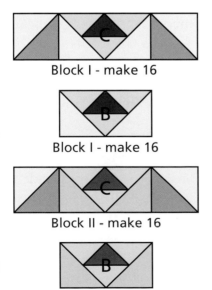
Block I - make 16

Block I - make 16

Block II - make 8

Block II - make 16

Block II - make 16

Diagram 1

3. For Block I, sew a B section to opposite sides of an A section. (**Diagram 2**)

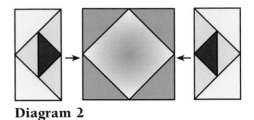
Diagram 2

5. Sew C section to remaining sides of A/B to complete Block I. Make eight blocks. (**Diagram 3**)

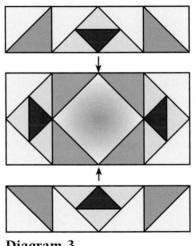
Diagram 3

6. Repeat steps 3 to 5 for Block II. (**Diagram 4**)

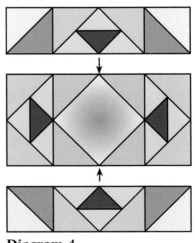
Diagram 4

6. Referring to layout, place blocks in four rows of four blocks each, alternating Blocks I and II.

7. Sew blocks together in rows. Press seams for rows in opposite directions then sew rows together.

8. Refer to How Do I Make a Complete Quilt?, pages 14 to 18, to add borders and finish your quilt.

Quilter's Gift Quilt Layout

QUILTER'S GIFT
BLOCK I PATTERN

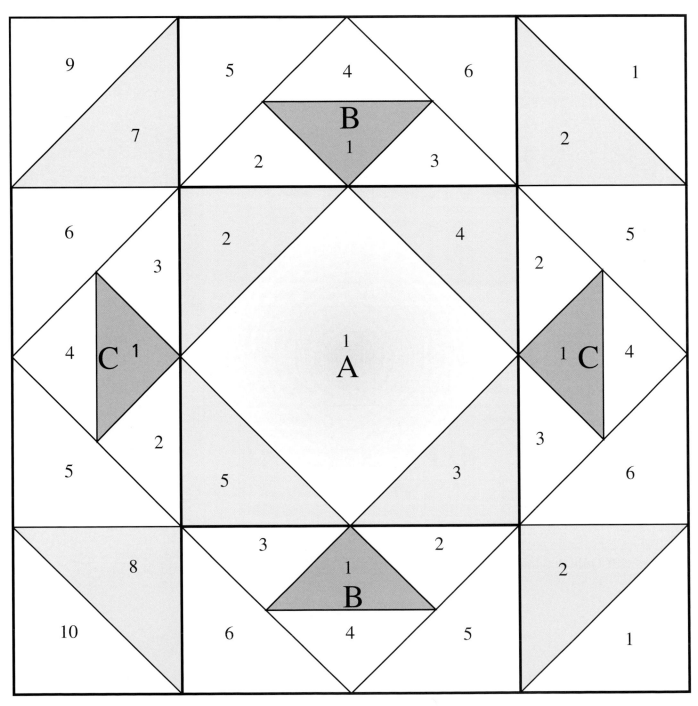

QUILTER'S GIFT
BLOCK II PATTERN

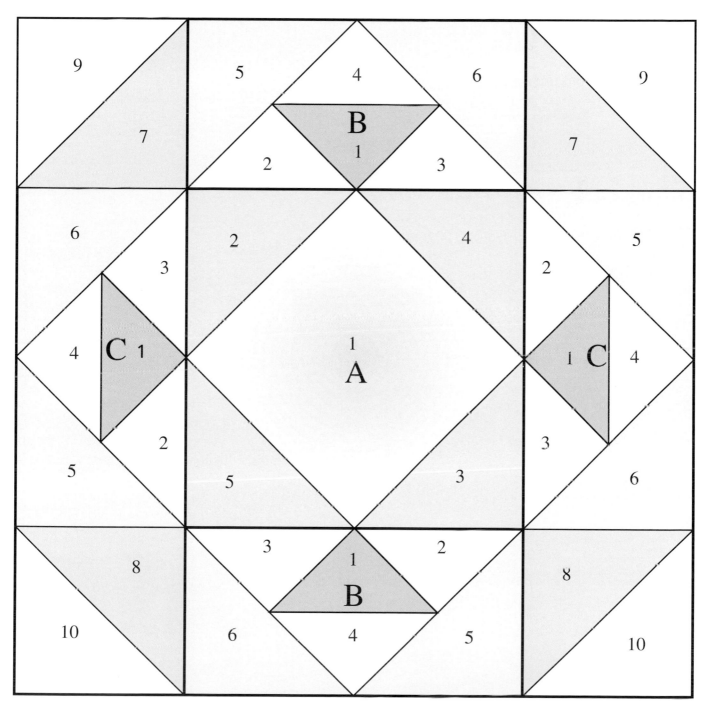

FLORAL MINI

Foundation Piecing is especially useful when making mini quilts; it eliminates cutting and piecing all of those tiny pieces. The foundation piecing makes sewing these small triangles and squares a breeze. In this tiny quilt, stars radiate through a miniature springtime flower garden.

Approximate Size: 18" x 18"
Block Size: 7" finished
Number of Blocks: 4

MATERIALS

Fat quarter each small floral print 1, 2, 3, 4

Fat quarter each dark turquoise and medium dark turquoise

Fat quarter each dark pink and medium dark pink

Fat quarter floral print (second border)

Fat quarter dark turquoise (first border)

Fat quarter backing fabric

Batting

CUTTING INSTRUCTIONS

For Foundation piecing, you do not have to cut exact pieces. To make it easier for you, however, I have given you the size to cut strips for each space. This will make piecing easier and may waste less fabric. If you prefer, follow the instructions on page 7 and cut fabric pieces as you sew.

Three 1⅜"-wide strips, medium dark turquoise (all space 1)

Two 1¾"-wide strips each, floral print (all spaces 2, 3)

Three 2¼"-wide strips, dark turquoise (all space 4)

Two 2¼"-wide strips, dark pink (spaces A5, B6)

Two 2¼"-wide strips, med dark pink (spaces C6, D5)

One 2¼"-wide strip, each floral print (spaces A6, B5, C5, D6)

Borders, Binding

Four 1"-wide strips, dark turquoise (first border)

Four 2"-wide strips floral print (second border)

Four 2½"-wide strips, binding fabric

INSTRUCTIONS

Note: Read How Do I Make the Block?, pages 9 to 14, before beginning.

1. Using pattern on page 101, make four foundations referring to How Do I Make the Foundation?, page 6. Cut foundation in four sections, then cut each section in half.

2. Starting with the upper left block, make sections A, B, C and D using Cutting Instructions as a guide. **Note:** *Use the same floral print in all light areas throughout block.* (**Diagrams 1, 2, 3 and 4**)

3. Sew section A to section B and section C to section D. (**Diagram 5**)

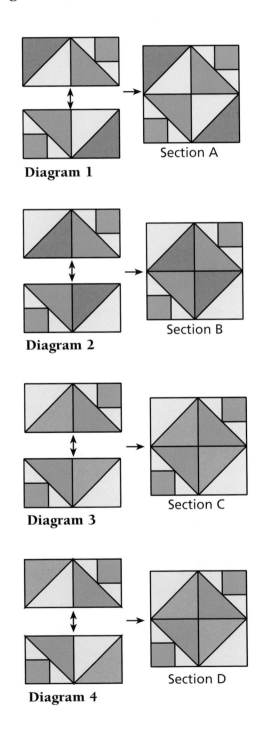

Diagram 1

Section A

Diagram 2

Section B

Diagram 3

Section C

Diagram 4

Section D

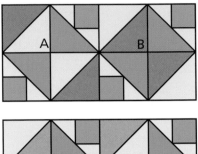
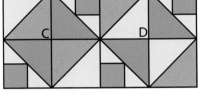

Diagram 5

4. Sew pairs together to complete block. (**Diagram 6**)

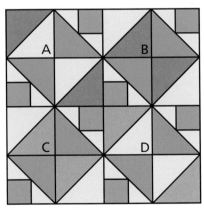

Diagram 6

5. Repeat steps 2 to 4 for three more blocks using a different floral print for the background of each block. (**Diagram 7**)

6. Sew blocks together in pairs. (**Diagram 8**)

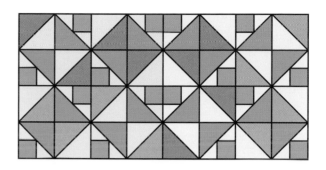

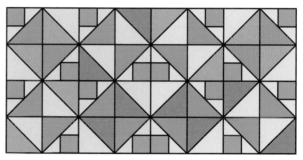

Diagram 8

7. Sew pairs together. (**Diagram 9**)

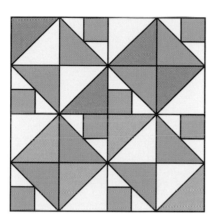

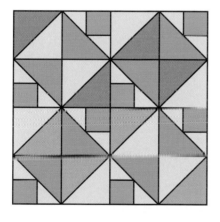

Diagram 7

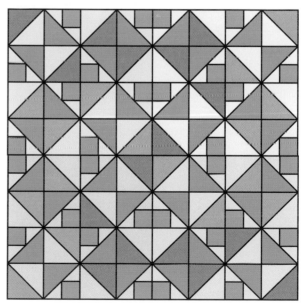

Diagram 9

8. Refer to How Do I Make a Complete Quilt?, pages 14 to 18, to add borders and finish your quilt.

Floral Mini Quilt Layout

100

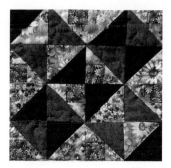

FLORAL MINI
BLOCK PATTERN

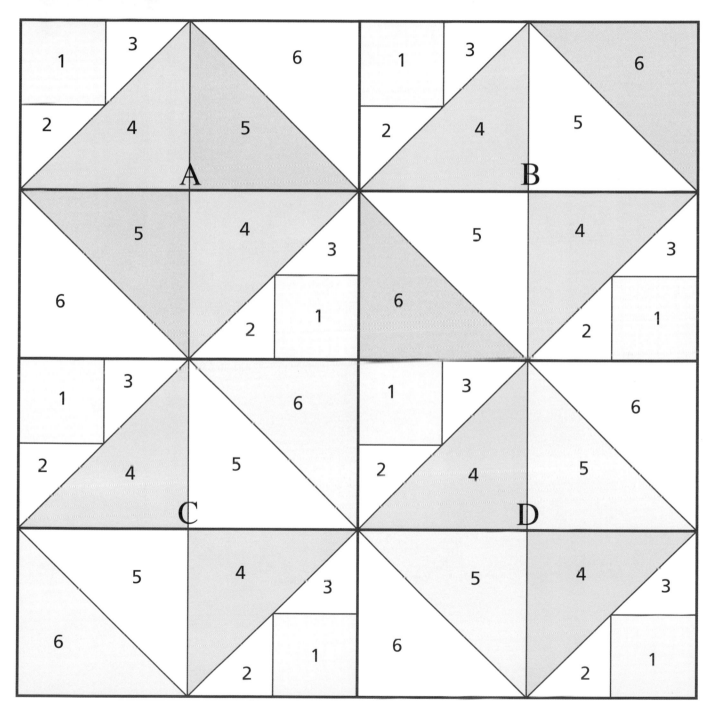

LOG CABIN STAR

One of the most popular of quilt patterns, the "Log Cabin," is easiest to create with foundation piecing. This simple "Log Cabin" block with carefully placed fabrics make this quilt an attractive addition to any décor.

Approximate Size: 57" x 69"
Block Size: 6" finished
Number of Blocks: 80

MATERIALS

3/8 yard red fabric
7/8 yard black/rose print
7/8 yard black paisley print
1 yard beige glitter print
1 1/8 yards beige/red print
1/2 yard red (first border)
3/4 yard black/rose print (second border)
5/8 yard binding fabric
3 1/2 yards backing fabric
Batting

CUTTING INSTRUCTIONS

For Foundation piecing, you do not have to cut exact pieces. To make it easier for you, however, I have given you the size to cut strips for each space. This will make piecing easier and may waste less fabric. If you prefer, follow the instructions on page 7 and cut fabric pieces as you sew. Refer to individual patterns, pages 108-117, for color placement.

Five 2"-wide strips, red
Ten 2"-wide strips, black/rose print
Twelve 2"-wide strips, black paisley print
15–2"-wide strips, beige glitter print

18–2"-wide strips, beige/red print

Borders, Binding
Six 2"-wide strips, red (first border)
Seven 3 1/2"-wide strips, black/rose print (second border)
Seven 2 1/2"-wide strips, binding fabric

INSTRUCTIONS
Note: *Read How Do I Make the Block?, pages 9 to 14, before beginning.*

103

1. Using patterns on pages 108 to 117, make foundations A through J referring to How Do I Make the Foundation?, page 6. (**Diagram 1**)

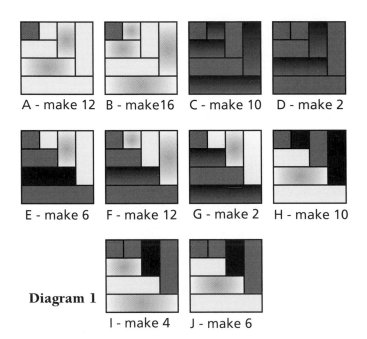

A - make 12   B - make16   C - make 10   D - make 2

E - make 6   F - make 12   G - make 2   H - make 10

Diagram 1

I - make 4   J - make 6

Hint: *For the steps 2 through 7, mark blocks to make placement easier when laying out quilt.*

2. Sew a Log Cabin A to a Log Cabin B noting positions; repeat. Sew pairs together for Block I. Make four Block I. (**Diagram 2**)

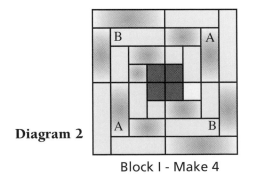

Diagram 2

Block I - Make 4

3. Sew a Log Cabin I to a Log Cabin A; sew a Log Cabin C to a Log Cabin F. Sew pairs

together for Block II. Make four Block II. (**Diagram 3**)

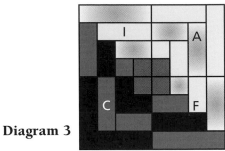

Diagram 3

Block II - make 4

4. Sew a Log Cabin B to a Log Cabin E; sew a Log Cabin J to a Log Cabin C. Sew pairs together for Block III. Make four Block III. (**Diagram 4**)

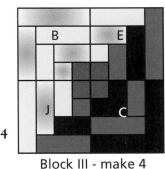

Diagram 4

Block III - make 4

5. Sew Log Cabin B to Log Cabin G; sew a Log Cabin H to a Log Cabin D. Sew pairs together for Block IV. Make two Block IV. (**Diagram 5**)

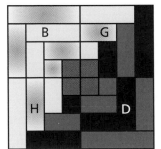

Diagram 5

Block IV - make 2

6. Sew Log Cabin J to Log Cabin B; sew a Log Cabin C to a Log Cabin E. Sew pairs together for Block V. Make two Block V. (**Diagram 6**)

8. For top and bottom border rows, sew four Log Cabin H alternating with four Log Cabin F; repeat for seven more pairs. Sew four pairs together to complete one border; repeat. (**Diagram 8**)

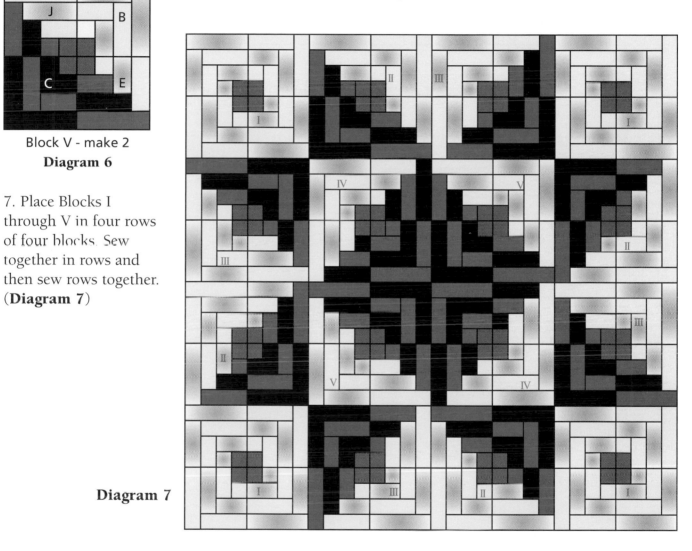

Block V - make 2
Diagram 6

7. Place Blocks I through V in four rows of four blocks. Sew together in rows and then sew rows together. (**Diagram 7**)

Diagram 7

Diagram 8

Border - make 2

105

9. Sew borders to top and bottom of quilt. (**Diagram 9**).

10. Refer to How Do I Make a Complete Quilt?, pages 14 to 18, to add borders and finish your quilt

Diagram 9

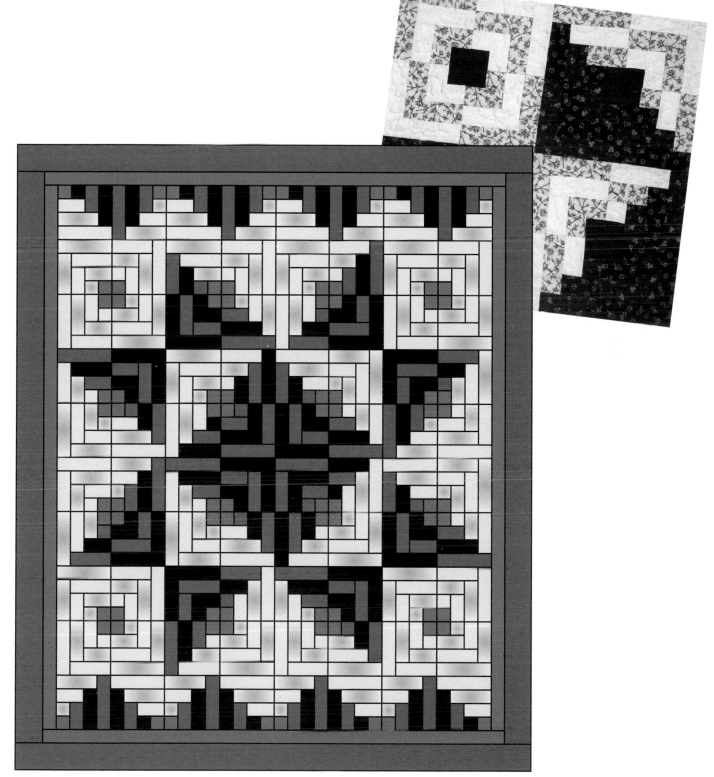

Log Cabin Star Quilt Layout

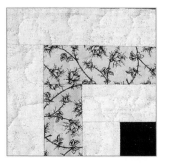

LOG CABIN STAR
BLOCK A PATTERN

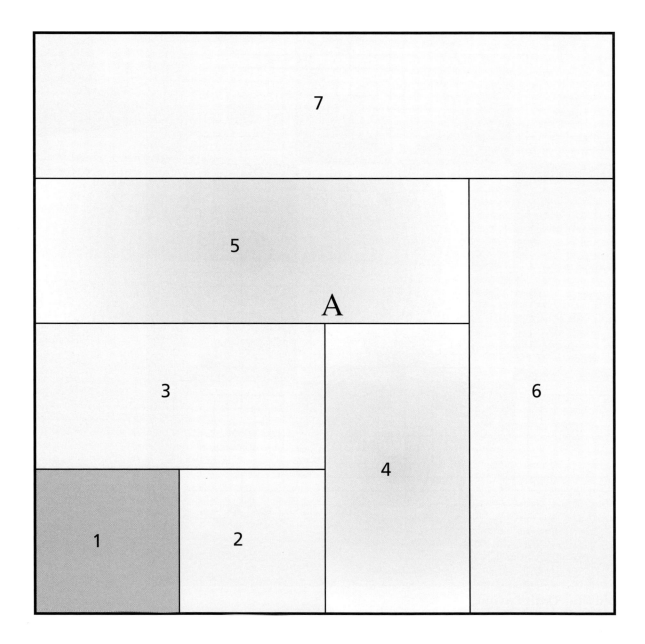

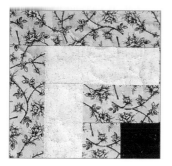

LOG CABIN STAR
BLOCK B PATTERN

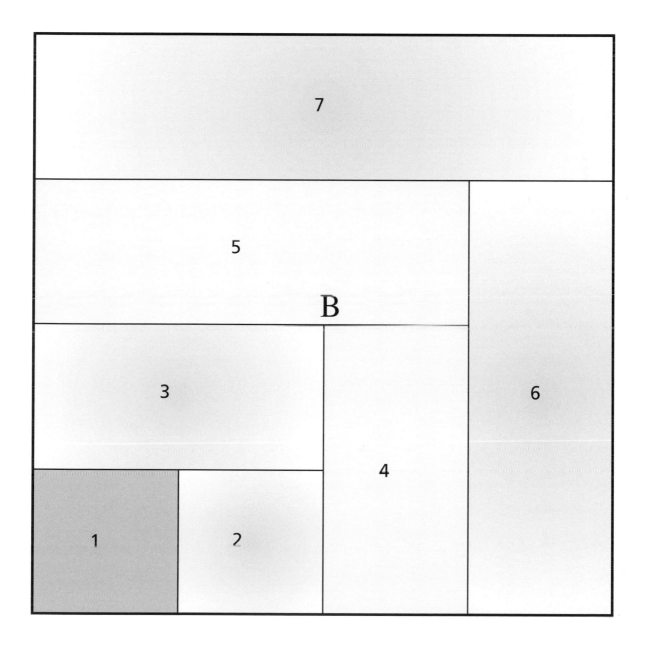

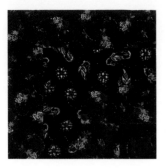

LOG CABIN STAR
BLOCK C PATTERN

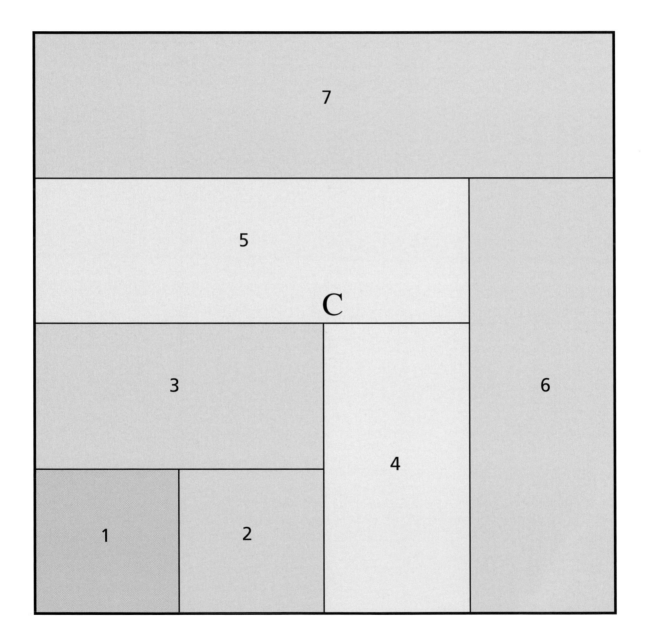

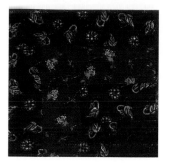

LOG CABIN STAR
BLOCK D PATTERN

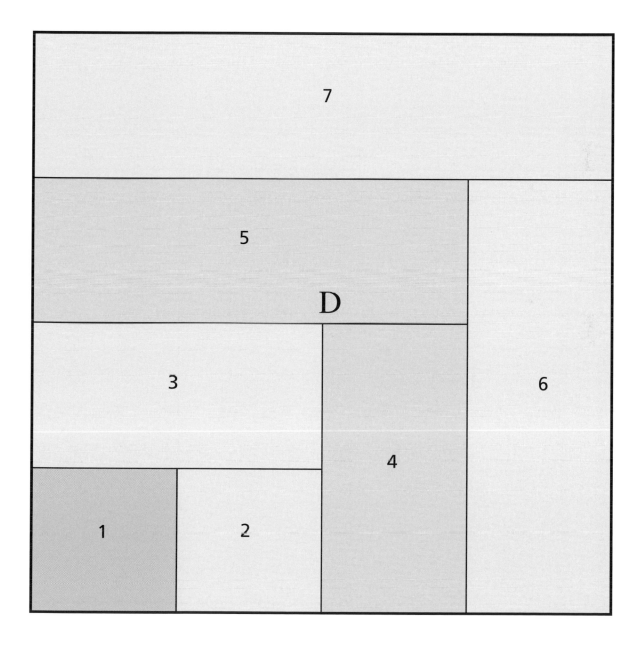

LOG CABIN STAR
BLOCK E PATTERN

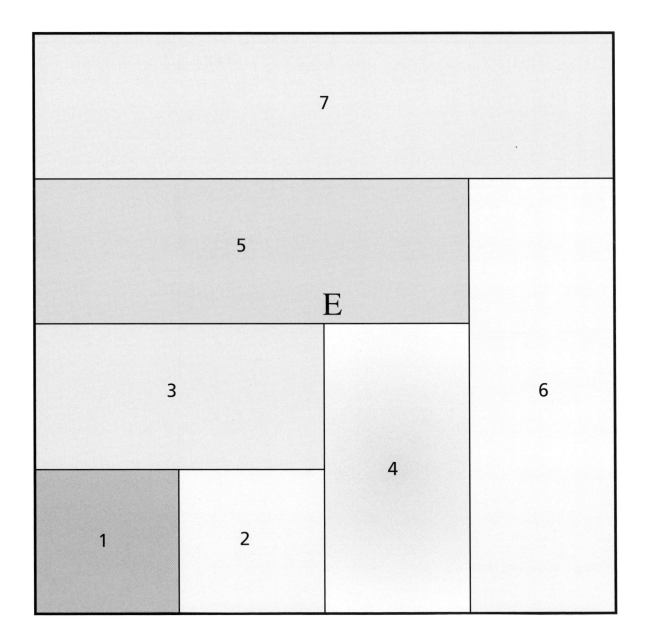

LOG CABIN STAR
BLOCK F PATTERN

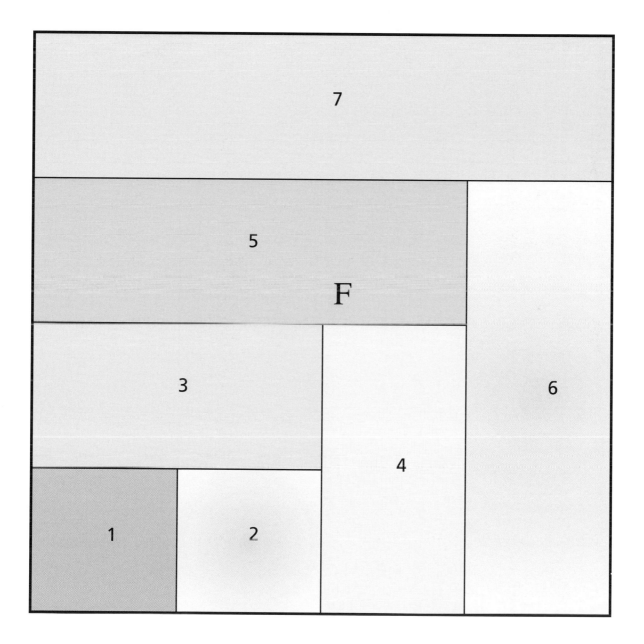

LOG CABIN STAR
BLOCK G PATTERN

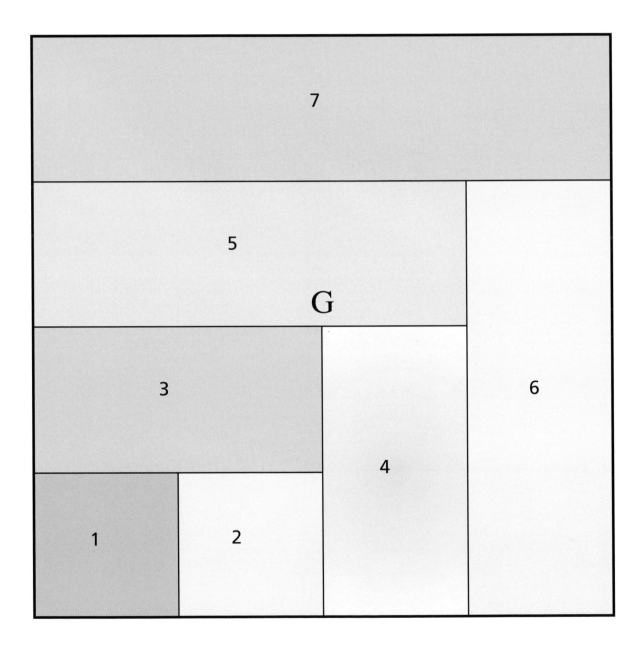

114

LOG CABIN STAR
BLOCK H PATTERN

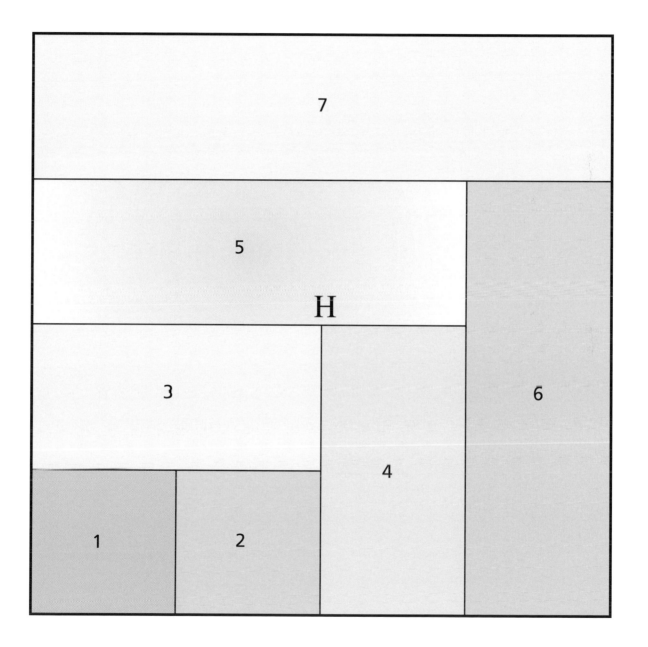

LOG CABIN STAR
BLOCK I PATTERN

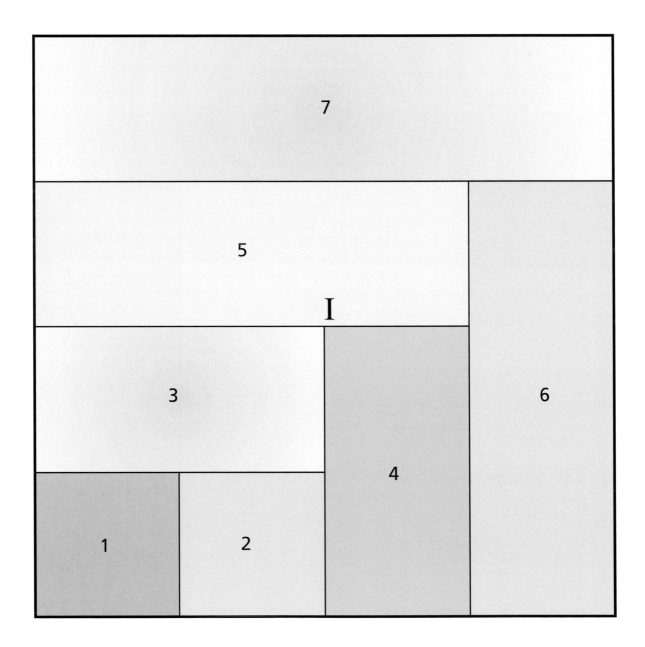

LOG CABIN STAR
BLOCK J PATTERN

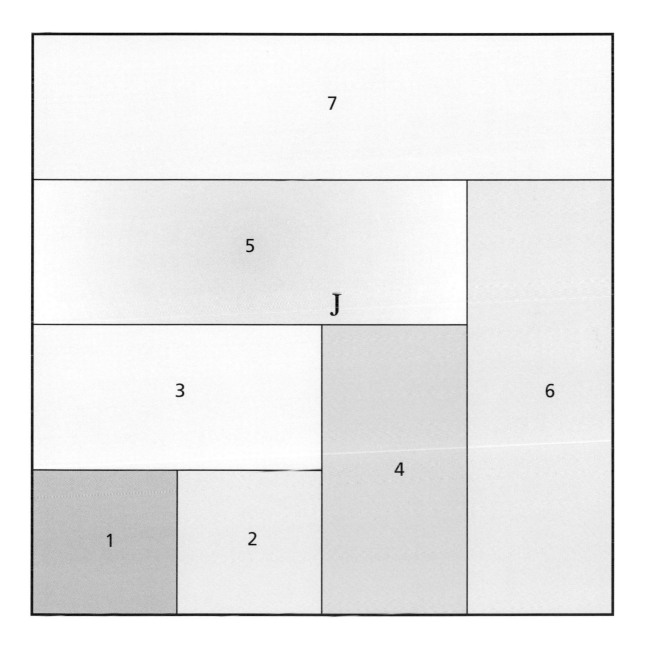

CURVY KALEIDESCOPE

Imagine making curves by sewing straight lines! That's just what you are doing when you make this stunning quilt made with Ricky Tims's new fabric line Convergence for FreeSpirit®. While this is a more advanced foundation-pieced quilt, careful sewing will make it easy to do.

Approximate Size: 37½" x 37½"
Block Size: 7" finished
Number of Blocks: 16

MATERIALS

1½ yards dark red swirl
2¼ yards purple swirl print
2 yards green swirl
⅜ yard dark red swirl (first border)
⅝ yard multi print (second border)
½ yard binding fabric
2½ yards backing fabric
Batting

CUTTING INSTRUCTIONS

For Foundation piecing, you do not have to cut exact pieces. To make it easier for you, however, I have given you the size to cut strips for each space. This will make piecing easier and may waste less fabric. If you prefer, follow the instructions on page 7 and cut fabric pieces as you sew.

Two 3"-wide strips, purple swirl (space 1)
Six 2½"-wide strips, green swirl (spaces 2, 3, 4, 5)
Three 2¾"-wide strips, green swirl (space 6)
Seven 2¾"-wide strips, purple swirl (spaces 7, 8, 9, 10, 11, 12)

Three 3"-wide strips, purple swirl (space 13)
Ten 2½"-wide strips, dark red swirl (spaces 14 to 21)

Borders, Binding
Four 2"-wide strips, dk red swirl (first border)
Four 4¼"-wide strips, multi print (second border)
Four 2½"-wide strips, binding fabric

INSTRUCTIONS

Note: *Read How Do I Make the Block?, pages 9 to 14, before beginning.*

1. Using the pattern on page 121, make 16 foundations referring to How Do I Make the Foundation?, page 6.

2. Make 16 blocks using the Cutting Instructions as a guide. (**Diagram 1**)

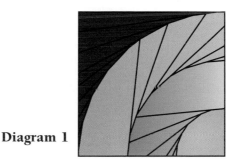

Diagram 1

make 16

3. Place blocks in four rows of four blocks referring to Layout.

4. Sew blocks together in rows. Press seams for rows in opposite directions then sew rows together.

5. Refer to How Do I Make a Complete Quilt?, pages 14 to 18, to add borders and finish your quilt.

Curvy Kaleidescope Quilt Layout

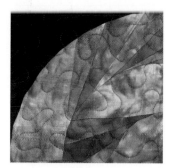

CURVY KALEIDESCOPE
BLOCK PATTERN

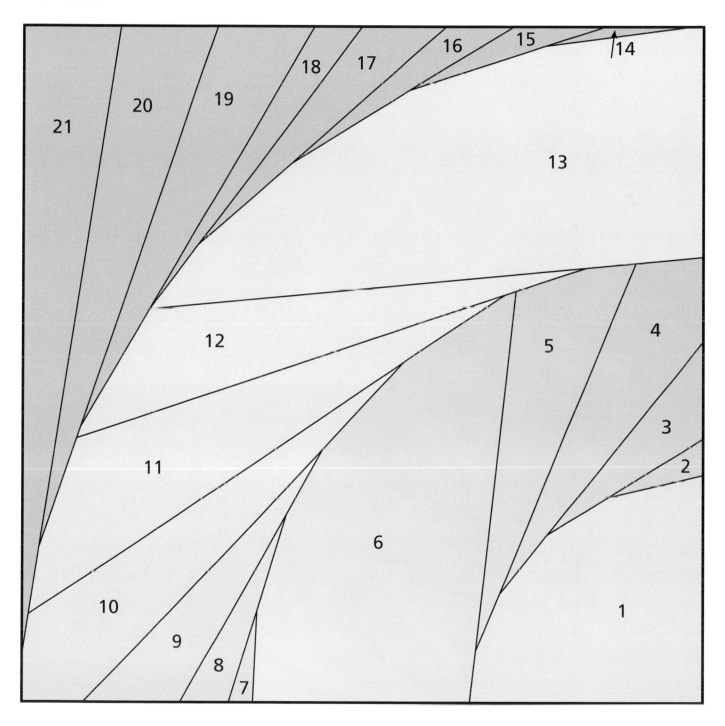

STARBURST CHAIN

Although a little more involved than many of the other quilts in this collection, this quilt only appears complex and difficult. Using foundation piecing to make this quilt will make matching seams easier than ever. The striking starbursts are linked together by a lush sage green chain.

Approximate Size: 86" x 106"
Block Size: 20" finished
Number of Blocks: 12

MATERIALS

2 yards dark green
2½ yards blue
1½ yards light green
1½ yards medium green
1½ yards terra cotta
3 yards light blue
⅝ yard light blue (first border)
1⅛ yards medium green (second border)
½ yard dark green (third border)
1¾ yards blue (fourth border)
¾ yard binding fabric
8 yards backing fabric
Batting

CUTTING INSTRUCTIONS

For Foundation piecing, you do not have to cut exact pieces. To make it easier for you, however, I have given you the size to cut strips for each space. This will make piecing easier and may waste less fabric. If you prefer, follow the instructions on page 7 and cut fabric pieces as you sew.

Section A

Ten 4¼"-wide strips, dark green (space 1)
Eight 2¾"-wide strips, blue (spaces 2, 3)

Section B

Four 3"-wide strips, white (space 1)
Four 3½"-wide strips, white (space 2)
Four 3½"-wide strips, blue (space 3)

Section C

Seven 2¾"-wide strips each, light green and
   medium green (space 1)
Eight 1¾"-wide strips, terra cotta (space 2)
Five 2½"-wide strips, white (space 3)

Section D

Four 3"-wide strips, dark green (space 1)

Three 3½"-wide strips each, light and medium green (space 2)

Three 3½"-wide strips, terra cotta (space 3)

Four 3"-wide strips, white (space 4)

Three 3½"-wide strips, white (space 5)

Three 3½"-wide strips, blue (space 6)

Section E

Four 3"-wide strips each, light and medium green (space 1)

Four 3"-wide strips, dark green (space 2)

Seven 3"-wide strips each, light and medium green (space 3)

Eight 1¾"-wide strips, terra cotta (space 4)

Six 3½"-wide strips, white (space 5)

Borders, Binding

Eight 2½"-wide strips, light blue (first border)

Eight 4½"-wide strips, medium green (second border)

Nine 1½"-wide strips, dark green (third border)

Nine 6½"-wide strips, blue (fourth border)

Four 6½" squares, terra cotta

Ten 2½"-wide strips, binding fabric

INSTRUCTIONS

Note: Read How Do I Make the Block?, pages 9 to 14, before beginning.

1. Using patterns on pages 127 and 128, make 48 foundations A, B, C, D and E referring to How Do I Make the Foundation?, page 6.

2. Make 48 of each block section (A, B, C, D and E). **(Diagram 1) Note:** *Make 24 C, D, and E sections with light green in spaces C1, D2, E1 and E3 and 24 C, D, and E sections with medium green in spaces C1, D2, E1 and E3.*

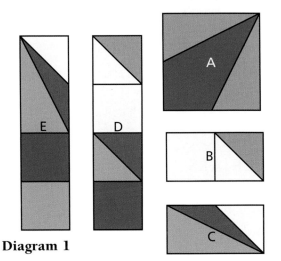

Diagram 1

make 48 of each section

3. Sew section A to section B. **(Diagram 2)**

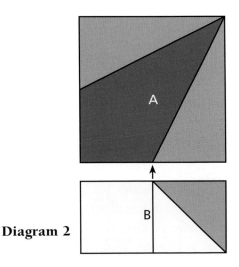

Diagram 2

4. **Note:** *For steps 4 to 7, use medium green sections C, D and E. Sew section C to section B.* **(Diagram 3)**

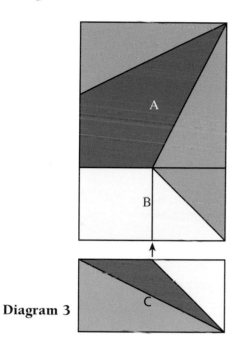

Diagram 3

5. Sew section D to section A/B/C. **(Diagram 4)**

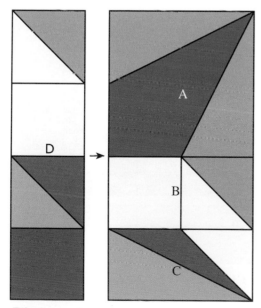

Diagram 4

6. Sew section E to A/B/C/D to complete a Starburst quarter block. **(Diagram 5)**

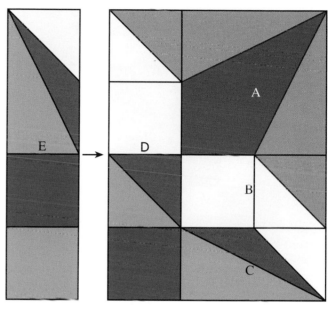

Diagram 5

7. Repeat steps 3 to 6 for 23 more quarter blocks.

8. Sew two quarter blocks together; repeat. **(Diagram 6)**

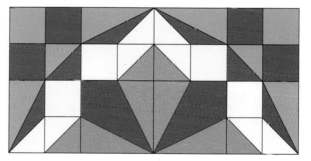

Diagram 6

9. Sew pairs of blocks to complete Starburst block. Make five more blocks. **(Diagram 7)**

Diagram 7   make 6

10. Repeat steps 3 to 9 for six Starburst blocks replacing the medium green with light green. **(Diagram 8)**

Diagram 8   make 6

11. Referring to Layout, place blocks in four rows of three blocks, alternating blocks with medium green and light green. Sew blocks together in rows. Press seams for rows in opposite directions then sew rows together.

12. Refer to How Do I Make a Complete Quilt?, pages 14 to 18, to add borders and finish your quilt. **Note:** *To add the last border, sew strips to sides first. Sew 6½" terra cotta squares to each end of remaining border strips and sew to top and bottom.*

Starburst Chain Quilt Layout

STARBURST CHAIN
QUARTER-BLOCK PATTERN

Note: *Make six blocks using light green in spaces C1, D2, E1, and E3 and six using medium green in spaces C1, D2, E1, and E3.*

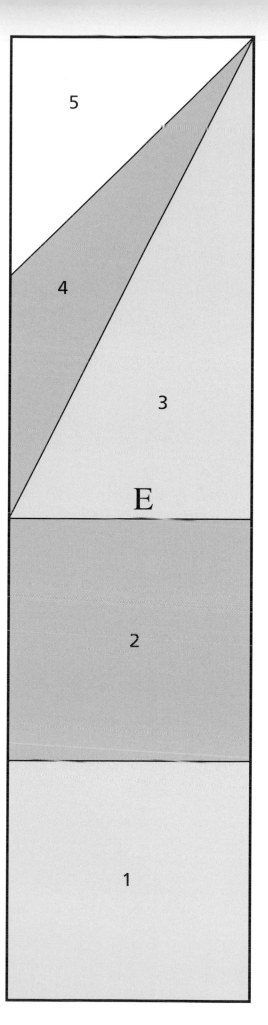

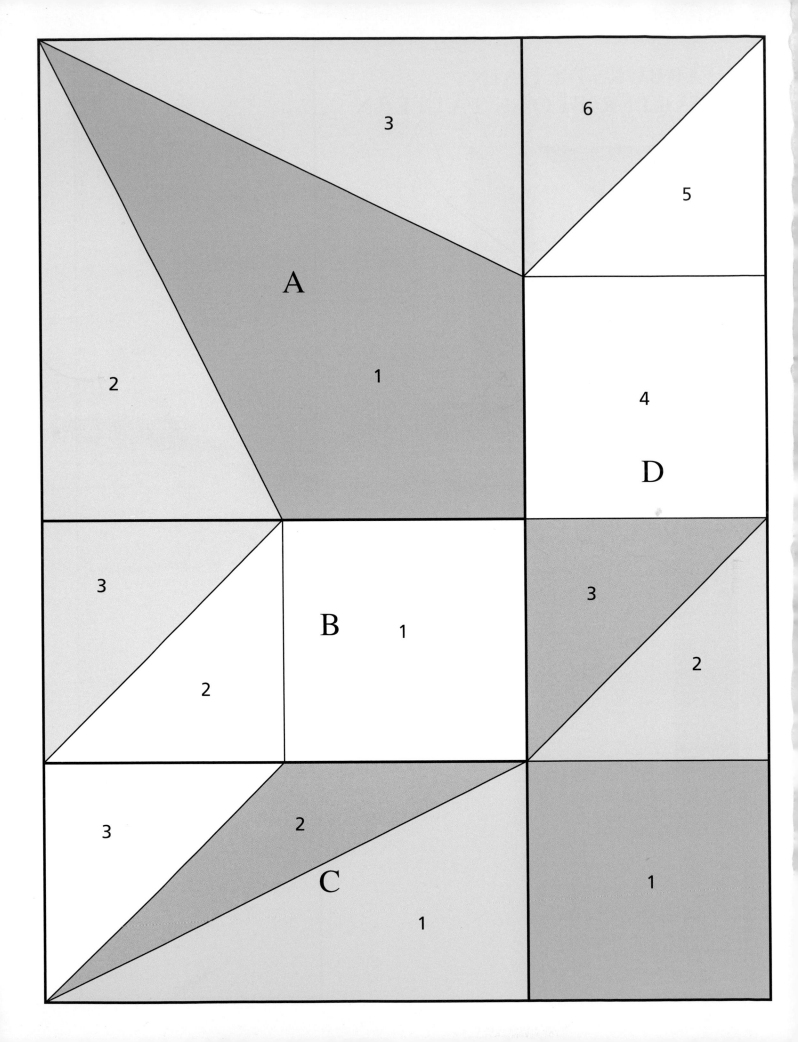